HUMBLE THE POET

HOW
TO BE
love(d)

**SIMPLE TRUTHS FOR
GOING EASIER ON YOURSELF,
EMBRACING IMPERFECTION
& LOVING YOUR WAY TO A BETTER LIFE**

HAY HOUSE, INC.
Carlsbad, California • New York City
London • Sydney • New Delhi

To The Lion & The Puppy,
We'll forever be family.

SCAN HERE FOR ACCESS TO A FREE GIFT THAT WILL ENHANCE YOUR READING EXPERIENCE.*

* For those, like my parents, who are going to ask me, "How do I scan?". . . Simply open the camera on your phone and point it toward my face in the middle of the funny box. You'll see a bubble pop up, tap on the bubble.

Copyright © 2022 by Humble The Poet

Published in the United States by: Hay House, Inc.: www.hayhouse.com®
Published in Australia by: Hay House Australia Pty. Ltd.: www.hayhouse.com.au
Published in the United Kingdom by: Hay House UK, Ltd.: www.hayhouse.co.uk
Published in India by: Hay House Publishers India: www.hayhouse.co.in

Cover design and cover art: Ruben Rojas
Interior Design: Nick C. Welch

Cataloging-in-Publication Data is on file at the Library of Congress

Tradepaper ISBN: 978-1-4019-7422-0
E-book ISBN: 978-1-4019-6991-2
Audiobook ISBN: 978-1-4019-7037-6

10 9 8 7 6 5 4 3 2 1

1st edition, December 2022
2nd edition, December 2023

Printed in the United States of America

This product uses papers sourced from responsibly managed forests. For more information, see www.hayhouse.com.

CONTENTS

DIAMONDS FOR PAPERWEIGHTS: A LOVE STORY viii

   0.   HOW TO MAKE ANYBODY AND EVERYBODY FALL IN LOVE WITH YOU . . xiv

WTF IS LOVE?

BLANK CHECK: A LOVE STORY 2

   1.   LOVE IS A PATH, NOT A DESTINATION 6

   2.   BIG L LOVE VS. SMALL L LOVE 10

   3.   LOVE ATTRACTS LOVE 14

   4.   PERFECT IS THE ENEMY OF LOVE 19

   5.   LOVE AND EGO WON'T HOLD HANDS 22

   6.   SECRETS DON'T HELP LOVE 28

   7.   LOVE DOESN'T JUDGE 32

   8.   TO LOVE ONE IS TO LOVE ALL 36

   9.   WHY WE THIRST FOR LOVE 41

  10.   YOU CAN ONLY HAVE UNCONDITIONAL LOVE FOR 45

  11.   LOVE THE VERB > LOVE THE NOUN 49

NAZR: A LOVE STORY 52

LOVE FOR SELF

LONELY DANCES: A LOVE STORY 58

  12.   OUR ADDICTION TO APPROVAL DENIES US LOVE 62

  13.   HOW TO PUT YOURSELF FIRST WITHOUT BEING SELFISH 66

  14.   LOVE IS NOT IMPRESSING OTHERS, IT'S IMPRESSING OURSELVES . . . 71

  15.   LOVING YOURSELF IS BEING YOUR OWN BEST FRIEND 75

  16.   LOVE IS FORGIVING YOURSELF 79

  17.   SELF-LOVE MEANS KNOWING WHAT MATTERS 84

  18.   ENVY PULLS US AWAY FROM LOVE 89

  19.   LOVE YOUR FLAWS AND INCOMPLETENESS 94

  20.   LOVING YOURSELF IS BEING YOUR OWN NURTURING PARENT 98

  21.   LOVE IS BREAKING OUR CYCLES 103

22. LOVE IS FEELING IT ALL .107
23. LOVE IS ALWAYS TELLING THE TRUTH . . . TO YOURSELF 111
24. SELF-CARE IS NOT ALWAYS SELF-LOVE 116
25. BE KIND TO YOUR INNER CRITIC 120
26. PROGRESS IS A GREAT FRIEND OF LOVE 124
27. LOVING YOURSELF IS HONORING ALL OF YOURSELF 127
28. LOVE YOUR TRUTH > YOUR RELATIONSHIPS 130
29. LOVE IS SITTING WITH PAIN 136
30. LOVING YOURSELF IS KNOWING WHO YOU ARE 144
31. LOVE IS PUSHING YOURSELF . . . SOMETIMES 148
32. LOVE IS COMMUNICATION WITH OUR DEEPEST SELF 152
33. LOVE IS SAYING NO 155
34. LOVE IS SHOWING YOUR TEETH 159
35. BE WHAT YOU LOVE, NOT WHAT LOVES YOU 164
36. LOVE IS KEEPING YOUR COMMITMENTS TO YOURSELF 169
37. THEY CAN ONLY LOVE US FOR YESTERDAY 173
38. LOVE WHO YOU ARE AND THE EXPERIENCES THAT SHAPED YOU . . .177
39. WHAT'S IN YOUR WALLET?? 180

LOVE FOR OTHERS

365 PROPOSALS: A LOVE STORY **186**
40. THE CRAZY SHIT WE BELIEVE ABOUT LOVE 188
41. DON'T FALL IN LOVE WITH POTENTIAL 193
42. LOVE IS FUEL, NOT GLUE 197
43. MIXED SIGNALS MEAN NO 204
44. INTERDEPENDENT RELATIONSHIPS >
    CODEPENDENT RELATIONSHIPS 209
45. THE CURE FOR LONELINESS 214
46. LOVE IS A GOOD FIGHT .220
47. LOVE NEEDS TO BE RECEIVED 224
48. LOVE IS ABOUT SETTING INTENTIONS, NOT EXPECTATIONS 229
49. LOVE WITH YOUR EYES OPEN 234

50. LOVE IS EXPLAINING AND ACCEPTING YOUR FLAWS 238
51. RELATIONSHIPS WE BUILD > RELATIONSHIPS WE HAVE 242
52. LISTENING IS LOVE 247
53. LOVE IS ATTUNEMENT .255
54. CONFLICT STYLES 260
55. LOVE IS A GAME, AND GAMES SHOULD BE FUN 266
56. IS HONESTY A PATHWAY TO LOVE? 270
57. WALLS AND WINDOWS 275
58. JEALOUSY IS NOT THE RIGHT SIGN OF LOVE YOU'RE LOOKING FOR . .279
59. NICE GUYS DON'T FINISH LAST 284
60. WHEN TO CLOSE PATHWAYS OF LOVE
    (WHEN TO END RELATIONSHIPS) 288
61. A BROKEN HEART IS AN OPEN HEART 294

YOU DON'T KNOW LOVE: A LOVE STORY **298**
62. THE LAST BOOK I'LL EVER WRITE 302

ABOUT THE AUTHOR 307
ACKNOWLEDGMENTS 308

DIAMONDS FOR PAPERWEIGHTS:
A *love* STORY

I was supposed to practice this, write out a full pros and cons list, and read that "How to break up better" ebook from a relationship coach I researched. I didn't get a chance to do any of it. I had no exit plan, no one was yelling, there wasn't going to be a storming off, no doors would be slammed, no one was lost in the heat of the moment.

Instead, all I could do was look at the patterns of the rug, but now I couldn't describe them if I wanted to. The shapes were moving as tears filled up my face. The puppy looked at me and realized this was an opportunity to grab tissues out of my hand. She probably loved the taste of the salt of my tears, how fitting.

I didn't go there to do anything or say anything. I hadn't made my peace with ending it, but I had been thinking about ending it for weeks, if not months, if not years. She spoke about the lessons she was learning during our "break" and was asking if I was open to seeing a couples therapist, who could possibly provide us with the tools we needed to make it through the rough patch we were going through.

I didn't say anything, and she knew.

She asked, "Have you made a decision?"

All I could do was keep my head down and look at the rug, skin itchy from the puppy,* envious that she had no idea how horrible the moment was. The puppy and I played tug-of-war with a bandanna as I tried to pick the right words.

My mind was playing words of wisdom on a loop:

Decency is the absence of strategy.

The goal here can't be to avoid looking like the bad guy. The goal is to be as honest and open as possible.

"I'm scared to hurt you. I'm scared I wasted your time. I'm scared of hurting my mom and letting everyone down. I'm scared to prove your sister right. I'm just scared."

I looked up at her for a second. She was crying. I saw the most gut-wrenching pain on her face. And when her eyes met mine, it got worse.

Even with the pain, she was being so kind. That's a special kind of strength.

"You have to decide and do what's right for you. Maybe we can just take more space; I feel like I've been making so much progress. . . ." She paused and I could feel her negotiating and then stopping herself. "But then again, we've taken space, and if this is what you need to do, then decide that."

She didn't want to hear the words but wanted to hear the words.

I wanted to say, "I'm sorry, this needs to be over," and get up and walk out, but I was terrified. I still wasn't sure, and I didn't want to throw it all away.

---

*   When the fuck did I get allergic to dogs?

Don't deny your future by holding on to your past . . . . Shut the fuck up! Please, just shut the fuck up. This is not a time for inspiring quotes, this is real life, real people, real consequences, real pain. Just shut the fuck up, please!

"I just don't want to break up our family. When I see her, I see you, she is you," she said, looking at our puppy. The puppy really was me—feisty with moments of cuteness, she walked to her own tune and played by her own rules. "I can't look at her without seeing you."

My heart crumpled, and my eyes continued to fill up.

She was trying her best not to guilt me into staying. She was trying her best not to make me feel bad. She wasn't thinking about herself, she was thinking about me. She didn't have a petty bone in her body. She told me our relationship had no deal breakers and that she would always stick with me, even when I thought I didn't deserve it.

I tried my best to keep it about me. I wanted to tell her that although she loved me so intensely and unconditionally, I wasn't able to receive or honor it. Instead, I had been treating her love as a free pass to do dumb shit without consequence, but there's always consequences. I needed to work on myself so I wouldn't do that dumb shit anymore, not so I could be in a healthy relationship, but just so I could live with myself.

"I hope at least one percent of you is relieved," I said.

"Zero percent of me is relieved," she replied quickly.

Tears and tissues piled up. She wasn't mad at me, she wasn't begging me to stay, but she was so sad. I never wanted to make her this sad. I felt like a piece of garbage for doing this to her.

"Just make your decision and go," she said.

When I went to get up off the floor, I could see the pain in her face go from a 10 to 5,000 as she looked up at me with those eyes, and I was paralyzed.

Earlier in the year, she had looked up at me with those same eyes, tears filling them up as she awkwardly went down on a knee in the water off the beach and gave her version of a proposal: no ring, just her, in her ultimate vulnerability. I was confused until I saw all of our friends with their phones out, excitedly recording the moment.

"I was supposed to have a necklace for you, it was my dad's, but it wasn't ready in time, and I don't want you to see this as pressure, but I mean, we're here."

I said yes, and I meant it.

Now I'm standing over her, about to walk away from my fiancée, my partner, the one person who has consistently loved me more than I love myself.

If you knew her, or had even just met her, you would have realized how lucky I was to have such abundant love in my life, but unfortunately, no one can fill our hearts if our doors are closed.

I didn't start writing this book because I'm an expert on love— far from it. I'm writing this because I'm desperate. Desperate to realize love, accept love, and learn how I keep fucking it up. Desperate to know why I had a rare diamond the size of my fist, but treated her like a paperweight, a placeholder, out of sight, doing nothing to encourage her to shine. I didn't hold space for her to be her beautiful self, leaving us both exhausted, defeated, and alone. Alone not because I'm by myself, but because I don't enjoy my own company.

I want to figure this love thing out; I want to be worthy of it. I want to appreciate and be aware of it, especially when it walks up and smacks me in the face. I don't want to learn how to make someone fall for me, or how to craft a perfect text message to leave them wanting more, or how to get noticed. I don't care who pays, or what not to say or wear on a first date.

I care about love, how to love, and how to be loved.

If we dig to the root reason of why we do anything in our lives, it's because of love. We want it so bad that we're willing to design our entire lives around chasing it. We lose ourselves in the love stories of others, and daydream about the "what if" love stories from our pasts. There are a billion songs, books, poems, and movies about love. We assigned the most important organ in our body to it, the heart, even changing the shape of it to make our hearts more beautiful, perfect, and symmetrical to look at. It's not the beauty of our hearts that keeps us alive, it's that work it does. Our hearts are asymmetrical, slimy, and not nice to look at. But our hearts are consistent, hardworking, and they keep everything else going.

Our hearts aren't perfect, and the games we play around love aren't fun.

Something's gotta change.

Love is simple, but not easy, and the deeper I went on this journey to better understand, practice, and realize love, the more I learned that it was about letting go of the old, outdated ideas instead of trying to gain new ones. We don't realize how much shitty love advice has been passed down to us through media, culture, religion, and our own DNA.

Love isn't something we just achieve, it's something we have to do, become, practice, and explore. The more we can be a source of love, the more love will be experienced, both in and around our lives.

This book wasn't a labor OF love, but a reminder that it's a labor TO love. I began taking a deep dive into the world of love after getting engaged in hopes of becoming a better partner and eventual husband. Instead, the journey turned me inward and made me realize I couldn't continue down this road without drowning and taking her with me. Many of the things I thought were love never were, and even more things I avoided confronting ended up being the only things I needed to realize more love in and around my life.

Here I am, presenting the most expensive piece of work I've ever created. Not expensive in terms of the price you paid to read it, but the price I paid to write it.

This book isn't full of hollow quotes and empty ideas that will look nice on social media. Instead, it's full of useful thoughts and practical tips to bring love back out into the sun.

More than showing you how to be loved, I want to show you how to *be love*.

Although I got up to walk away, I didn't end up leaving that day, but that's a story for another page.

Let's get into it.

0.

HOW TO MAKE ANYBODY AND EVERYBODY FALL IN LOVE WITH YOU

Yeah, right, this isn't that type of book.

The real title of this chapter is "TLDR: WTF Is Love?"

You may have only bought this book because everyone was talking about it, and you had no plans to actually read it after posting a picture of it in your lap alongside a warm cup of tea and some beautiful scenery in the background.[*]

For those who only purchased this book because it matched the aesthetics of their bookshelf, I wrote this chapter for you, so you can grasp the gist of this book and still sound interesting at parties when it comes up in conversations.

I promise I wrote this chapter sober.[**]

---

[*]   Shelfie culture is a real thing.

[**]   Unless we count caffeine as a drug, which we definitely should.

A misquote to Rumi summed it up best: "Out beyond ideas of wrongdoing and rightdoing, there is a field. I'll meet you there. When the soul lies down in that grass, the world is too full to talk about."

Love is that field.

You see, we simplify the world in terms of duality, meaning things are either *this* or *that*: good/bad, happy/sad, right/wrong, hot/cold, up/down, black/white. Looking at the world like this came from our early years when our brains were still forming; our simple minds had to view life in a simple way. We carry that simple dualistic view of life into our adulthood, even as we are able to grasp life as something more complex.

Love is the simplest form of that complexity.[*] It's the experience beyond duality.

> ## *"Love is what remains when all other emotions are gone."*
> ## — Naval Ravikant

This is why so many equate love to God, because like the idea of God, love is nothing and everything at the same time. It's the beginning and end of it all—the source.

This book isn't about showing you some mystical secret to finding that source, it's to remind you that you've always been that source; it's just that the choices we make, informed by all the things we've been taught and shown, can often make us forget that. **Forgetting that we are the source of love has us looking everywhere else but the one place where love is experienced the most, within.**

---

[*]   How's that for an oxymoron?

We have to let go of the idea that we have to be ENOUGH or WORTHY or DESERVE love; these measurements don't apply to us. You can have enough money, get enough sleep, eat enough food, and even then defining *enough* is hard.

Being enough of a person? That's not a unit of measurement that applies. Love isn't a roller coaster with a height restriction, or an R-rated film requiring you to be a certain age to watch it. Stop wondering if you're enough, and realize there's no such thing as enoughness when it comes to you.

Love doesn't have to be earned or found, it just has to be realized.
We don't have to add anything to our lives to experience love, but rather the opposite. We have to clean out the clutter of outdated beliefs, ideas, and understandings of love. Much of that comes from religion, society, rom-coms, and tribal thinking.

The biggest chunk of this book is to help us see those ideas and choices in our behavior, recognize the patterns, and make better decisions moving forward.

The people we love in our lives are really the people that show us where love is, and we create pathways between them and us to experience more love. This gives us the freedom to love everyone.

Some pathways will be easier than others, some wider and more dependable. Others may only remain open for a moment, and that's okay.

What we do serves to open or block these pathways. Observing ourselves will allow us more opportunity to decide how much that breeze of love flows in our lives.

Learning to create those pathways of love with ourselves will do wonders to create and strengthen pathways with others. That's not just an idea, it's work. Often very obvious and boring work; it's not trips to Ubud, Naples, and Delhi;* it's a trip inside to view and accept all that is there.

Love as a verb is far more important than love as a noun. To realize and experience love is to practice and share it.

I am a schoolteacher, and I will reinforce the most important ideas in this book by revisiting them, because very rarely do we read something once and have it stick with us forever—keep that in mind as you flip through these pages; if it's worth sharing, it's worth repeating.

Now, back to making everyone and anyone fall in love with you.**

---

* This is a reference to *Eat, Pray, Love*, which I only read to impress a girl.
** Evil winky emoji

LOVE DOESN'T HAVE TO BE EARNED OR FOUND, IT JUST HAS TO BE REALIZED.

BLANK CHECK:
A *love* STORY

"$800! That's how much I paid for the car to begin with! This was supposed to be, like, $150 max to fix!"

I was a student and didn't have a lot of money. I couldn't afford it.

"When I gave it to them to fix, they found other problems, so we had to take care of those," my dad replied.

When I wasn't home, my father had my shitty $800 Plymouth Sundance towed to the shop to get fixed. I had been trying to find my own hookup on repairs, but he was tired of waiting and did it himself, and now I was stuck with the bill.

I was livid.

The argument got out of hand. I didn't like that he'd done this behind my back, and he didn't feel he needed to justify his choices, in his house, to his son.

As the argument grew, things got off topic, and the next thing I heard my dad say was, "If you don't like it, get out."

"Fine," I said, and I ran to the basement and grabbed a bunch of garbage bags. I ran up to my room and started filling the garbage bags up with clothes. I called a friend and told him I needed him to pick me up.

My dad hadn't expected me to react this way, but we were both stubborn guys cut from the same cloth. I could see he was surprised, and now that I was leaving, my mom and sister chimed in.

"Stop being dramatic," my sister said.

My mom was confused, half upset and half worried that I was about to leave. I grabbed my garbage bags and headed for the front door. She stood in the way. I ran to the back door, trying to squeeze the bags through the narrow entrance.

My father came out and said, "Don't leave."

And I stubbornly replied, "You already told me to."

My father stood by the backyard gate, so I threw the bags over the fence, hopped it, and ran across the street toward the parking lot where I'd told my friend Harjot to wait.

Years later Harjot still tells the story of seeing me running toward him with all these garbage bags, jumping in the car screaming, "Go! Go! Go!" as if I had just robbed a bank and needed to make a getaway.

For the next week, I crashed on couches, slept on floors, and floated around Toronto at any friend's place that would take me. My plan was to leave the city and get to a smaller town where I could stay with a friend longer term. I didn't have a lot saved up but figured I could get a job doing anything.

I was all in, really not expecting to ever go home. I cared about being right more than I cared about keeping the peace and picking my battles. I was too upset to listen to anyone in my family. None of them seemed to care about what happened, they just wanted me back home, but there was no way I was going back home when I didn't feel heard.

Almost two weeks into things I got a call from my sister.

"Mom's not eating anymore. I'm not telling you what to do, but I thought I'd let you know."

"I just don't think it's fair that no one listens to me in that house. I didn't do anything wrong this time," I replied.

"Well, if you want to talk to Dad, I'm sure he'll talk to you now."

I had a brief conversation with my dad over the phone. It wasn't pleasant, but we were both doing it for my mom. I came home, and my father pretty much avoided saying anything to me for the better part of a year. He pretended I wasn't there and said nothing to me when I was around; we were like two antisocial strangers occupying the same space.

Eventually time went on and things went back to normal between us. We never had a conversation about the fight.

That was 15 years ago.

Recently, when I was having dinner with my sister and my teenage niece, my sister jokingly brings up the story. "I totally forgot, but you ran away once," she said. That piqued my niece's interest. She loves hearing stories about how bad we were as kids.

I retold the story in an amusing tone, highlighting the garbage bags more than the argument.

And then my sister chimed in. "I don't think you know this, but once you left the house, Dad gave me a blank check and told me if you called to give you anything you needed."

It took time to soak in what she'd just said, but it's always been that way with my father. **Love wasn't spoken, it was only acted on.** He knew I was him, and he was me, and I really wasn't coming home. Instead of trying to change my mind, he decided to try to take care of me from afar. My father, like most people from his generation, had limited tools when it came to expressing love and communicating. None of that changes the fact that he's a parent, and no matter the generation, their priority is keeping their children's well-being always front of mind.

1.

LOVE IS A PATH,
NOT A DESTINATION

It seems like everyone is "looking" for love, like it's hiding in that secret Harry Potter cupboard under the stairs.[*] We decide if we can't find love, it's because of our shortcomings or lack of worthiness, but really it's because we don't realize it's been under our noses the whole time.

Media teaches us that everything will pay off in the end. The endings of our favorite films generally involve characters living happily ever after, and we assume that's what they do until they die.

We start to apply this view to our own lives, adding milestones to our timelines that we think we have to hit, not realizing that real life is much more cyclical, and cycles repeat without a happily ever after.

We have to graduate from high school, graduate from college, get a job, get a promotion, find a partner, have some kids, then help the kids finish school, get their jobs, get their promotions, find their partners, and the cycle of hitting milestones never ends. What we need to do is take a step off the hamster wheel and ask WHY am I working toward these things? What's the meaning behind all of this?[**]

---

[*]   My editor said this reference doesn't make sense; I haven't seen the movies, so don't judge me!
[**]   Other than having cool things to post on social media . . .

When we go a layer deeper on our journey, we'll see a common thread with all the things we chase: it's a promise of something at the finish line. When we become self-aware, we realize there is no finish line, so instead of trying to win the race, we should enjoy running it.

Robert Holden, Ph.D., coined the term *destination addiction* to mean "a preoccupation with the idea that happiness is in the next place, the next job, and with the next partner. Until you give up the idea that happiness is somewhere else, it will never be where you are." This destination addiction applies to love as well, especially when our understandings of and desires about love are heavily influenced by the media we see.

There is no finish line in love; we don't get the "happily ever after." Instead, we get another day and our credits roll only after we're dead. This means love is less of an achievement and more like a way to live. **Love is an action more than a reward, and to realize love is to act on it, service it, and receive it when it flows your way.** None of this requires a partner, a child, a lot of social media followers, or anything besides ourselves.

We can walk a journey of love with ourselves and with others, and the more we walk and work on it, the stronger it becomes. It's like a muscle. You don't go to the gym because you were born with big muscles; you go to the gym to grow muscles. That same idea applies to love.

The love songs are going to sell an idea that the right person will walk into our lives and with them will be an Amazon package full of love, and now that we've found love, we can live until we're gray and the only wrinkles in our lives will be on our skin. The inconvenient truth is that no one can give us any more love than we can give ourselves, and being on a voyage of life devoted to sharing as much as possible is really the best way to experience love.

There will definitely be moments when the love feels more potent, and oftentimes that's not even love. It's attention, validation, pleasure, and a whole bunch of other things that can temporarily feel like love but aren't the real thing. I get that when I go on tour, step on stage to a crowd that hoots and hollers at my presence, listens to my words intensely, and lines up for hours to get a book signed. It feels great, but none of it has much value if I don't prime myself daily to share, receive, and accept love; that will come from my choices and actions, not theirs.

Commit to a path of love, not a search for it. As I said in *Things No One Else Can Teach Us*,[*] "There is no pot of gold, the rainbow is the reward." Finding opportunities to express, share, and receive love is an ongoing journey that doesn't end until we take our last breath, and even then, the impact of the journey will have touched so many that the love that flowed in and around you will live long after you're gone.

---

[*] Waddup, book reference!

COMMIT TO A PATH OF LOVE, NOT A SEARCH FOR IT.

2.

BIG L LOVE
VS. SMALL L LOVE

There are levels to love, and we've felt it our whole life. They are different gestures, sizes, and depths. My friend Aubrey Marcus, an experimentalist, unconventional fitness junkie, and human optimizer, differentiates it as "Big L love" and "Small L love." Big L love is that all-encompassing, change-your-life rush of emotion that fills every part of your being kind of love, and Small L love is the quick fixes of attention and affection we chase to make up for our lack of Big L love.

Small L is our love for ice-cream sundaes, and Big L is our love for the way our grandmother's wrinkly, soft hands feel on our face first thing in the morning. Big L compounds over time, gets deeper, and becomes our foundation, while Small L is just a hit that has us wanting more, always leaving us depleted shortly after.

Small L love is the low-hanging fruit, the immediate gratification—the validation, attention, and admiration: think all of the things we get from social media, winning an award, or having a wedding. It's the external stuff that we think is love. Not only do we chase it, we often believe we have to do and be something to earn it. Once we get it, it rarely feels as good as we'd hoped, so we chase some more.

Big L love, well that's the love that finds us. That's the love that sweeps us away the first time we hold our baby niece and see the universe in her eyes. It's the rush and overwhelmedness we feel and wonder, *What did I do to deserve something so abundant?*

Big L love doesn't have to be earned, only realized. Big L love isn't spread, it's tapped into. It's the love we all crave, and when we can't find it,[*] we settle for the Small L love.

Big L love makes us feel more and do less, while with Small L love, we're constantly chasing new hits, new sources, thinking at any moment that if we can feel it one more time, one more victory, one more win, we'll finally feel satisfied, but we don't.

I don't even need to write these out for you to know what I'm talking about. The Big L is what inspired your favorite song, and its absence is what wrote your favorite tragedy. Small L love is the carrot that's constantly dangled in front of us to live at the bidding of others. It keeps us in line, contributing to the economy, and always feeling like we're just not enough.

Small L love gives us pleasure, Big L love gives us peace. Big L is what the religions promise us and what Disney movies have packaged so well to sell.

Small L is the flowers we give; Big L is the compassion and empathy we share. Small L is attachment; Big L is connection.

Our chase for Small L blocks our path to Big L, so let's be aware of the difference when we devote our energy to sharing and spreading love in our lives. With that said, we're human, and we're most definitely allowed to chase some of those Small L treats. Just make sure you know the difference and enjoy them in moderation.

---

[*]   Or won't do the work to discover it.

We can be in love with the idea of being in love without ever really feeling love, and that leads us down a blind, winding path toward all the Small L love. The Small L love will always come from outside of us, while the Big L love will always be within. If we spent less time chasing and more time allowing, we would realize how much of a source of this beautiful Big L love we can really be.

There are no rules to earning the Big L love other than to reduce the things that block it, whether they are our insecurities, expectations, short-term gratifications, or outdated beliefs. We don't achieve Big L love, we realize it, open pathways to it, and graciously accept it.

Know the difference and choose wisely.

SMALL L LOVE GIVES US PLEASURE, BIG L LOVE GIVES US PEACE.

3.

LOVE ATTRACTS LOVE

I, like you, deal with anxiety on a daily basis. Some of it feels silly, but most of it feels completely justified. What I learned was that much of my anxiety related to the future. I was worried about someone returning a text, a project getting completed, a future that seemed uncertain. I thought there was a solution and it was to simply "stop worrying," as if there was a magic light switch somewhere behind my head or under my ribs, and I could be happy-go-lucky forever.

I never found that switch.

In a conversation with a therapist, I had my anxiety framed as feeling an emotion for something that hasn't happened and may never happen. I was feeling the rejection from a person before I even asked for a favor, and then feeling too scared to ask the question. As a kid I failed the exam in my mind before I even took it, and that clouded my ability to study. We get anxiety around work, relationships, and being in new environments. That anxiety is like having a flat tire, and our anxious reactions and choices are us slashing the other three. When things are bad, our decisions can make them worse.

Don't get me wrong, there's anxiety around death, trauma, and abuse that haunts us, and it needs to be addressed for healing, but outside of the intense stuff, we have to realize that feeling anxiety about a bad thing that hasn't happened increases the chance of that bad thing happening.

I'm painting my future in the exact way I'm worried about.

If I'm scared, I'm attracting more fear.

If I'm angry, I'm attracting more anger.

If I'm suffering, I'm attracting more suffering.

It's a self-fulfilling prophecy. What I've only realized recently is that the solution to any problem shouldn't begin with the word STOP, It should begin with the word START.

Instead of *stop worrying* I need to *start* something. Remember, love is a verb; let's always focus on the action.

This principle that our feelings attract more of the same doesn't just apply to the unwanted feelings in our lives, it also applies to the wonderful experiences— happiness, joy, peace, and love.

So if we want more love, we have to START feeling and accessing more love first, because that in itself will attract more love.

This is an important idea to marinate on because for so many of us, when we think about wanting love, it's coming from a place of thirst, a place of fear, a place of scarcity. We don't feel like we're worthy of love and make self-deprecating jokes about being alone forever, not realizing that even those jokes impact the direction of our life.

We have to realize that love could come up and bite us on the ass and we wouldn't notice because we've isolated ourselves in a prison of unwanted emotions. We're afraid we won't "find" love, not realizing it's the fear itself that blocks the love touching our lives. **Love isn't found, it's realized.** Instead of finding a source of love, we need to realize the source of love that we are, and when we put that out into the world, more love will be attracted.

As Joe Dispenza says, "If you want to find your dream partner, write down all their qualities, and become them."

What we are is what we attract. This principle is universal, and it empowers us to have and become all that we can be. **When we love ourselves, we'll find love in others.** When we find love in ourselves, we'll stop looking for love in other places, and instead more love will be easier to realize. This means loving who you are now, but also loving your future. Instead of spending time worrying about potential bad things in the future, START falling in love with an awesome future you can envision.

I'm trying my best not to sound woo-woo "law of attraction"-ish, but it's completely true that how we feel decides where we go. Thinking in terms of scarcity, thoughts like, *There's never enough, I'm not enough*, will always mean there won't be enough, and you'll never feel like enough. Thinking in abundance—*I love and am loved*, and there's plenty to go around—helps make that true. We always have control over our attitudes and efforts, and this is a great place to direct them.

We don't realize how often we play the tapes of misery in our past and future and then are surprised when misery is what we get. I don't blame anybody for doing this; many of us have had to survive some bullshit, and that becomes a part of our story and a central idea to who we are, but it doesn't have to be. **We don't feel pain because we think about our shitty past, it's the opposite. We revisit our shitty past because we're already in pain.** Let's actively, intentionally, and regularly focus on feeling wonderful, and our memories and future projections will fall in line.

This isn't going to happen overnight, but neither did your ability to walk, talk, or read. It'll happen slowly over time, baby step by baby step, and it'll be a never-ending journey. We can always go deeper with love; there is no finish line, and there shouldn't be. Let's commit to START doing what it takes to stay in love with a future that hasn't happened, and let's feel love when we think about our past. Then we will become a magnet for love, and in this case, it isn't opposites attract.*

You know this principle of painting our future with our present emotions is true because that's every moment of anxiety you've ever had. So now, instead of "stop worrying," let's "start loving" so we can paint over the fear, pain, suffering, and anxiety that we thought was inevitable.

I'm not going to guarantee you that you'll find your soulmate in two to five business days by doing this; I'm going to promise you that, by keeping this up, you won't care either way.

---

*   Love has no opposite, but that's another chapter.

LOVE ISN'T FOUND, IT'S REALIZED.

4.

PERFECT IS THE ENEMY OF LOVE

You don't have to be perfect to be loved. That's it. That's the chapter.

We all can relate to not feeling like we're enough. It's why we do the things we do.[*] But some of us haven't realized that we've been striving to be perfect before allowing ourselves to experience love.

It sounds hyperbolic, but it's obvious when every time we do something less than perfect we get hard on ourselves and label ourselves unlovable. Who would want to love a piece of garbage like us? The problem is we reduce ourselves to only those two options: perfect or a piece of garbage. Please realize that perfect is the enemy of love, and when we scrap trying to be perfect, we also scrap feeling like a piece of garbage who doesn't deserve to be loved. What's left is an imperfect being who, despite being imperfect, can love and be loved.

Remember: you are so much more than what you do. We're a culture of hyper-productivity and comparing how much we're doing and achieving to others, even if all that doing and achieving adds little nutrition to our lives.

Loving ourselves despite being imperfect isn't a big stretch. Everyone we love is imperfect. Your ugly baby nephew who spits up all the time, or your best

---

* Including buying this book!

friend who has bad posture, or even Beyoncé, who has a four-minute compilation video on YouTube dedicated to her falling down stairs, off stages, and other places when gravity wasn't her friend.

Waiting for ourselves or circumstances to be perfect before we let love in damages our ability to love, whether it's yourself or someone else. Perfect doesn't exist; it never has, it never will, and **there's no such thing as being deserving or undeserving of love.**

There's been so much focus on perfection because the idea sounds nice. It's why we hope for it in the mirror, demand it of our role models, expect it during our weddings, and fake it for our social media feeds. But easier than demanding, expecting, or faking perfection is realizing that it serves no purpose other than deluding us further away from love.

Real love isn't honoring what's perfect, it's embracing all that's imperfect. Nobody I love has a symmetrical face or flawless skin, nor do they always say the right things, but I embrace those things as what makes them unique, or completely normal. I'm not perfect, but I'm grateful that I realized it's not important to seek or even strive for perfection in any way. When we chase perfection, we subtly tell ourselves we're not good enough as is. We hold grievances against who we are and create conditions for who we need to be in order to experience love from ourselves or the world. Holding this mindset will keep us in a never-ending loop of feeling like we're not enough, and that makes little sense considering we don't do that to anyone else. Letting go of the impossible standard of perfection creates a lot more room for love to breathe. It's okay to want to be better, but be mindful of the steps you take to get there. **Focusing on progress instead of perfection is sustainable, and also gives us opportunities to go deeper with the love we have.**

We love Beyoncé despite all the falls, and that love for her is why she always gets back up. Let's do the same for ourselves.

REAL LOVE ISN'T HONORING WHAT'S PERFECT, IT'S EMBRACING ALL THAT'S IMPERFECT.

5.

LOVE AND EGO
WON'T HOLD HANDS

I grew up in a household of Sikh heritage. Sikhi is one of the five largest faiths in the world and is most commonly associated with people who wear turbans, but it's so much more than that. The word *Sikh* means "student," and its big ideas are much richer than simply focusing on our outward appearance; it's a way of life. Sikhi explores our relationship with the truth/divine/god/source/almighty algorithm and sees lust, greed, attachment, anger, and ego as the distractions that take us further away from this relationship. As a kid I wasn't taught this initially and like in most faith-based education for kids, I was taught important names, dates, locations, and magical stories. It wasn't until I hit middle school that I was exposed to the bigger picture.

At 11, I could understand anger, greed, and attachment on the surface level. Even though there was a cooties pandemic[*] and girls were covered in them, I was beginning to wrap my head around lust as well. It was EGO that was the tricky one, even to this day. The younger me could only see EGO as pride.

All I knew was that ego is the big boss at the end of the video game of life.

---

[*]   Too soon?

Ego can be defined as our self-esteem and self-importance, but if we go deeper it can be seen as our sense of self in general. A great perspective on ego I recently came across is that **ego is defining ourselves by everything we're not,** and then trying really hard to protect that horrible definition.

Our natural need to feed and protect our ego locks in the idea of who we think we should be, keeping out many of the things we really are. That lack of authenticity means a lack of love. This is why our reputations serve as prisons. These prison walls disconnect us from others as well. We know this because in those moments when we feel intense love for someone or something, those walls start to come down, and we almost begin to blend together. Love turns the "you" and "me" into "we," and that experience is strongest when we're being our authentic selves, not who we think we should be.

Love melts the ego.

Ego is the border between you and me, it's the membrane between the drop and the ocean, it's the reason we look at all of creation and consider it more than one thing. Ego is what makes us consider ourselves separate from everyone and everything else.

Ego has a language—fear—and it's always whispering in our ears, telling us that we are in a fight for our lives. It needs to protect the ME, which means it has to ignore the WE. Even though the ego is self-indulgent, it requires all its food from outside validation. It's the ego that chases the gratification and the validation, that sees others as competition, and that wants to consume as much as possible because it always feels lacking.

The choices we make to feed and massage our ego do little to open pathways of love in our life. Our ego acts and reacts like a little toddler: impulsive, irrational, and difficult. It's the reason we get ourselves in trouble and find challenges connecting with others.

When our ego decides our self-worth, everything and everyone is a competition. Our ego needs us to accomplish goals to feel worthy, while love simply wants us to enjoy the journey. Ego is always pushing us to *do* more and *be* more to fulfill this perfect image of who we believe we need to be, while self-love requires us to accept ourselves as we truly are.

It's not love that breaks hearts. It's egos, and we all have them, and they're not going anywhere. All we can do is be mindful of the choices we make and the directions we head in and ask, "Are these choices opening up more pathways of love, or just feeding our forever-hungry egos?"

The lust, anger, greed, and attachment are all colors of the ego and ways it manifests itself. Recognizing this, and working to identify them in ourselves, makes more room for love to be realized. Our egos aim to serve ourselves, which further isolates ourselves from others, which will make it harder to connect and realize pathways of love.

To love is to be in love, and adding ego to the mix is to think we can only love someone else as something separate from us, like a trophy or a tool. It's the idea that we can hold ownership over others. With ownership comes control, and with control comes fears, anxieties, and insecurities. All of those unpleasant feelings only exist in the past and future, further robbing us of the present.

In the greatest moments of our lives, the most authentic experiences of love we ever had, there was very little ego in the room.

The origins of my name HUMBLE came from my recognition that ego can be the enemy, but even being humble in itself can still be from a place of the ego. I'm not here to ask you to destroy your ego, I'm here to ask you to pay attention to when you're doing and saying things to feed that ego, and instead make it a priority to embody choices that take you farther away from ego stroking and more toward opening pathways of love.

Before reading this book, you've already had experiences where your ego got the best of you and did damage to a relationship. Our ego is the one that makes us feel like we're constantly under attack and need to fight. It's the reason we react instead of respond; it's the reason we count likes and read comments and want to be more than we already are.

Things that feed our ego are highly addictive, and that's why most businesses and media are created around trying to satiate that insatiable appetite.

It's easy to spot the idea that owning a sports car or a $5,000 purse is just ego feeding, but it gets trickier when we get into more new-age ways of wellness.

A lot of modern spirituality that's come into Western society from the East has found success because it tickles our ego. The idea that the universe conspires for us, that we can manifest the life we want, that we should take deep dives into our astrological natal charts and understand why Cancers and Scorpios are perfect matches—all of this stuff is fun, but don't lose sight that it's there to tickle the ego more than to open pathways for love.

Being a vegan is love; endlessly telling people you're a vegan is ego.

Original spiritual beliefs were based on sacrifice of self to realize god/love. That meant service to others, building self-awareness,[*] and other ego-melting gestures. From a spiritual perspective, killing our identities brings us closer to

---

[*] Aka calling yourself out on your bullshit

love and the divine. For Sikhs, turbans were meant as a uniform to make us everyone and no one, much like an army shaving heads. Dissecting our sense of self is important to connect with others, and that means spending less time doing things that create a border between you and me.

There's no peace when we serve the ego, and that's why we chase so much pleasure to medicate that lack of peace.

Ego chases the delicious, while love focuses on what's nutritious.

I have an ego just like you, and every day I try to see the differences in my choices to see if it's being fed. My ego is the reason I like talking to pretty girls, or want to have a best-selling book, or want to be able to afford a dream home.

Love is having a full heart even after your shirt is covered with your child's vomit. It's cleaning up the neighborhood without recording it for social media. It's prioritizing connection over self-worth.

I'm no longer 11, but I'm still wrapping my head around this idea of ego. There are levels of ego, just as there are levels of love, and I hope you embark on the journey to go as deep as possible.

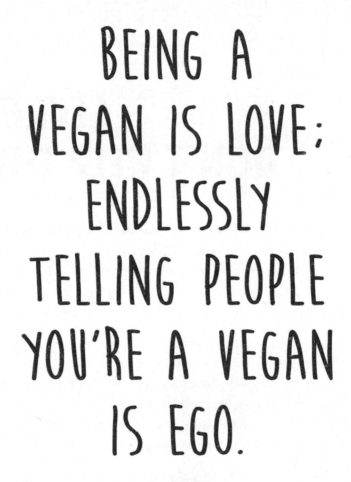

BEING A
VEGAN IS LOVE;
ENDLESSLY
TELLING PEOPLE
YOU'RE A VEGAN
IS EGO.

6.

SECRETS DON'T HELP LOVE

We all have secrets. My front teeth are fake.[*] Some secrets are bombshells, while others can be tiny white lies that have just snowballed into something bigger. Some people hide their true hair color or age. Others hide second families. Secrets come in all shapes and sizes, but no matter the size, holding on to and hiding them can become taxing.

According to a study done at Columbia University, the average person has around a dozen secrets, almost half of which they've never shared with anyone. Our secrets can be everything from who we voted for, to desires we're embarrassed about, to issues with relationships, sex, cheating, and times we've broken someone's trust. Some people keep their sexual orientation a secret, or don't want to share challenges they face around addiction and drug use.

It's hard work keeping a secret. It gets exhausting having to think about what to say, trying not to slip up, avoiding others when the topic arises. This stress chips away at our well-being, hurts our health, and affects our satisfaction in our relationships. The stress of hiding secrets can also feed anxiety, which in and of itself will increase symptoms of poor health.

---

[*] No, really, they were knocked out when I was 10.

The longer we keep hiding the secret, the bigger the consequences we fear for having it. It's one thing for people to find out our secret and judge us on it, but it's another for them to find out we were hiding something from them and judge us because of that.

Worse than hiding a secret is the fact that we have to be alone with those thoughts. No matter the size of a secret, it grows in our mind over time. Things randomly trigger thoughts about our secrets. We ruminate and mind-wander about those secrets, and that can be very harmful. Thinking about our secrets can make us feel like a fake, embarrassed, ashamed, alone, and isolated.

Not being able to tell others some of our heaviest thoughts is a form of social distancing. To hide secrets, we speak to others less, avoid conversations, give shorter answers, and reduce our chances of connecting with others. The more we're isolated with our own damaging thoughts, the more they chip away at our well-being.

Our secrets weigh us down, make us feel guilty, embarrassed, anxious, and paranoid. We keep these secrets at these expenses because we believe that life would be worse if the secret got out. I'm here to ask you to explore that maybe life would be easier if it wasn't a secret anymore.

There's value in expressing your secrets out in the open. Being able to talk plainly and without strategy makes life feel lighter. There's a lot of value to getting it off your chest, even if it's to just one person.

The fear of judgment isn't lost on me; it's normal to be concerned about what others think of us. But your own personal history has shown that good things can happen when you share yourself with others. The value goes beyond just getting to vent something you've been holding in, because sharing also pro-vides chances for emotional support, guidance, second opinions, and helpful advice other people can give you. This type of social support helps us feel more confident and capable in coping with the secret. Once it's been shared outside of ourselves, even to a single person, we'll think about it less, and feel less of a burden in holding on to it.

Remember, HAVING the secret is more work than HIDING it. It may not be very often that you'll have to maneuver in your conversations with others to hide your secret. But you'll always know you have one.

I'm not asking you to post about your breakup on social media,[*] or to tell 25 friends that you experienced sexual abuse, or to tattoo the amount of your debt on your forehead. I'm saying to see the value of getting it out to at least one trusted person, and if that can't be a friend, it can always be a professional, such as a therapist, who will keep everything you say confidential.

I've hidden debt, substance abuse, struggles with my mental health, and most other problems from my family and friends because I was afraid of their judgment and didn't think it was worthwhile sharing it. When I decided to let it all out, I was pleasantly surprised by the outpouring of love and support I received, and the lightness I felt for not having to hold these burdens alone. There are certain secrets in my life that only a friend or two know, and for that I'm grateful and it will bond us for life.

The longer we hold on to our secrets and bear them alone, the more crushing the weight will feel, and the less love we'll have room for. The guilt and shame of both the secret and keeping it from others does nothing to help us realize more pathways for love. It's not lost on me that some secrets can never be shared, but I implore you to relieve yourself of some of the tension and build real connections with others in the meantime.

Maybe one day I'll have the courage to share with y'all that I have beard implants.[**]

---

[*] Please don't vent on social media!

[**] I've said too much.

OUR SECRETS WEIGH US DOWN, MAKE US FEEL GUILTY, EMBARRASSED, ANXIOUS, AND PARANOID.

7.

LOVE DOESN'T JUDGE

I participated in a psilocybin mushroom ceremony, and it was intense.

I had already thrown up everything inside of me, and although I had volunteered to host the ceremony at my home, now in my distraught state, I wanted everybody out.

Who the fuck are these people and why are they in my space!

Quickly, a calm voice of reason kicked in,

You don't want everyone out.

You don't hate them, they're your friends. You're just feeling bad because you took too much medicine.

You've been here before and you're going to have to ride it out.

And so I did, away from everyone else, with our guide checking in on me every so often. I spent the better part of three hours pacing back and forth in the back room of my apartment, too overwhelmed to stop, unable to close my eyes and see all that there was to experience. My mind was a roller coaster of thoughts and emotions. There was a voice in my head telling me I was doing this wrong, and I should be with the group, meditating and reflecting on my intentions, instead of feeling like I was Keanu Reeves and I'd explode if I slowed down under 50 mph.[*]

---

[*] This is a reference to the film *Speed*, the single most repeatedly watched film of my life.

You're doing this wrong. You're ruining everyone else's experience. You didn't do enough prep. You're just thinking in circles. People are laughing in the other room, why are you freaking out? Why are you so weak?

Then my calm voice would chime in: *You're thinking this stuff because you took too much medicine, don't believe what you think, but pay attention to why you're thinking it.*

I was being both hyper-judgmental and hyper-insecure at the same time. Even after our guide came in to check on me a few times and told me I was perfectly fine to have the experience the way I was, his reassurance wasn't enough. The fact that I was in my own home wasn't enough, the thoughts of judgment and insecurity kept coming, and I was realizing why.

I needed to see the relationship between the two.

When we judge others, it's less about who they are and more a reflection of who we are. The judgments we place on others are often the same judgments we put on ourselves. There's nothing harsher we can say to others than the things we say to ourselves, and noticing the relationship between our judgments and our insecurities is the first step to addressing both.

Our best selves exist when our insecurities aren't present, because we can accomplish so much more when we're not busy judging ourselves. That thin layer of insecurity and judgment isolates us from others and can be bullet-proof glass, stopping the flow of love into our lives. To experience more love, we don't have to earn the respect of our judgmental side; we instead have to recognize that it can't be satisfied and to love our selves regardless.

We also have to realize that although we may think we're protecting ourselves, we're really imprisoning our true selves with these layers of insecurities and judgments. We still end up feeling embarrassed and that we're not enough. These extra layers of insecurity also make us feel more alone.

How do other people see us? That's an important question to ask. Most of the people in our lives see us from angles even we don't see. Sure they may not know our deepest, darkest secrets and flaws, but we don't know theirs either, and we can still love and accept them despite that.

We can all improve and strive for more, but that doesn't mean we can't feel good about who we are right now. **We judge because we're insecure and we're insecure because we judge.** The more we focus on loving others without judging them, the easier it'll be to love ourselves the same—that's the relationship between loving ourselves and loving others. The more we realize that our judgments of others relate to our judgments of ourselves, the more we can start breaking the pattern.

Who cares if you have a Rudolph zit on your nose—you've seen other people with the same issue and still accepted them. We have to realize we build the walls around us, and our judgments and insecurities are bricks and mortar.

Our journey of self-love is to work to judge others less and reduce how much we judge ourselves. We'll be more fun to be around, and we'll make more progress toward the life we want to live and the love we want to experience.

I want to thank the medicine for putting me in that unfamiliar and uncomfortable place to better understand myself and what I need to face. The medicine didn't make me more judgmental and insecure, it helped to reveal that it's always existed in the deepest parts of me. We can't heal what we don't reveal, and for that I am grateful to the medicine for bringing my deepest and darkest parts up into the light.

WE JUDGE BECAUSE WE'RE INSECURE AND WE'RE INSECURE BECAUSE WE JUDGE.

8.

TO LOVE ONE IS TO LOVE ALL

Years ago, in the jungles of Cusco, Peru, I was tripping the fuck out on ayahuasca. I had been double-platinum purging,[*] seeing colors and shapes, and feeling more terrified than a three-year-old in a room full of strangers.

In addition to the shamanic guides, there was a nurse in the room, and I turned to her and asked her to put me to sleep. "Give me anything, Nyquil, tranquilizers, let me sleep this off, this is too overwhelming."

Her cheekbones were so defined that from under the medicine she looked like a zombie from Michael Jackson's "Thriller." She spoke calmly in broken English. "It's okay, just focus on the love."

Frustrated, I replied, "I don't know what that means, just give me something."

She replied again, calmly, "It's going to be okay, just focus on the love."

What the fuck does it mean to focus on THE love, love isn't a stool in the corner I can stare at. It's not a sound I can turn my ears to.

---

[*]   It was coming out all ends.

The nurse then pulled out her 1950s blood pressure monitor, wrapped it around my arm, and checked me out. I was too wonky to see the numbers.[*] She looked at the dial, took the monitor off my arm, smiled again, and said, "I can't give you anything, just focus on the love."

At this point I realized I was on my own. My stomach was in pain from dry heaving. I couldn't figure out what was scarier, keeping my eyes open or closed. And I didn't want to have an accident in my pants.

I started repeating in my head, "Love love love love love love love love love love Mom."

My mother.

My mother's face popped up in my head, no expression, almost a portrait photo, and I began to calm down a bit.

In my head, I repeated: "Mom loves me, Mom is love, focus on Mom."

It took years for me to realize that my mother wasn't love, she's not even someone I love. Instead, my mother reveals a place where love is

We're not in love with anyone, we're just in love. The people are access points to that love that was always there. It's others that help us realize love.

But Humble, I *love* my mom, I *love* my partner.

No, my handsome friend, you just *love.*

We anchor our sense of love to a person. They serve as a spark for us to realize love, and because of that we get very deeply involved with them; but none of that means they're the source of the love. **People are pathways to love, doors to love.** Obviously some people are stronger pathways than others, especially if we've taken the time and energy to foster a relationship with them. But none of that means that losing them results in losing love.

---

[*] Not like I'd understand them anyways.

Everyone we come across serves as our teacher, revealing so much about ourselves and the world, we'd be very wise to pay attention. Just as loving someone is really having them reveal the places where our love is, being upset by someone is them revealing places where we're scared. We often dislike qualities in people that we dislike in ourselves.

Reframing the way we see our relationships with others frees us from the hostage situation that only one person is our salvation and path to love. We can have more pathways to love, unlimited pathways to be honest.

To know how to love someone means we know how to love everyone. Realizing more love is as simple as opening a bigger sail to catch more wind and traveling down more pathways—easier said than done, but nowhere near impossible.

Finding the good in people is finding more places where love peeks out its adorable head. This means we have to set aside judgment and choose curiosity instead. This means we have to dive into disagreements and confrontations with a better spirit. This also means we have to acknowledge and ACCEPT the flaws of others . . . which in turn will further allow us to accept the flaws in ourselves.

Yes, we are also pathways for love, for ourselves, and for others. And the wonderful way we treat others to get those pathways open is the same thing we can turn back upon ourselves.

I don't think I have the cultural clout to change I LOVE YOU to I FEEL LOVE WHEN I'M WITH YOU or I'M IN LOVE WITH YOU to I'M IN LOVE, but I hope this subtle shift helps you realize how abundant love really is in our lives, and that there are opportunities to realize more love everywhere. I'm not going to lie, some of the pathways will be easier than others, and with some people the door might get shut in our face, but with those experiences come newer learnings and wisdom to reveal even more love.

Pathways and access points to love aren't just people.

Love is revealed through play.

Love is revealed through ritual.

Love is revealed through work.

Love is revealed through community.

That evening, in the jungle of Peru, when prompted to focus on love I could have thought of ping-pong, stretching in the sunlight, Lauryn Hill's voice, a cute dog's Instagram page, or all of you awesome Beardos who connect with me every day.

I could have thought of the times I got lost in a poem, or the moment my niece could only hold on to my pinkie as we walked barefoot on the grass, or that time my sister posted, "I didn't know my brother was the next Edgar Allan Poe."

I could have thought of times my dog, Himmatt, put his head on my knee, or the times Lilly has said, "Of course, ryde or die, daawg," instead of saying, "You're welcome," when I thanked her for something.

I could have thought about the wrinkles on my grandmother's face, the tears in Sandy's eyes as the crowd in Boston sang "Happy Birthday" to me. I could have thought about bike rides, or the moment when I first held the first book I ever wrote in my hands.[*]

But I'm glad I thought about my mom because her pathway is always the most well kept, and her door opens the widest. With Mom, the love I realize seems more and more assured and abundant with every passing day.

There are access points to love everywhere. We can explore them, share them, and even be them. This takes off the pressure, melts the fear, and makes living with open eyes and an open heart so exciting.

---

[*]   Thank you for letting me go off on a tangent.

FINDING THE GOOD IN PEOPLE IS FINDING MORE PLACES WHERE LOVE PEEKS OUT ITS ADORABLE HEAD.

9.

WHY WE THIRST FOR LOVE

Los Angeles has a serious reputation for being full of flaky people. It's not that people lie to your face when they make plans—they may genuinely think it's going to happen—or maybe they're too afraid of looking rude by saying no. When the time comes for the plan to happen, they generally disappear with very little communication. It's so common here that when I go back to Toronto to visit, I'm always shocked at how reliable people are.

I realized this has to do with people not setting boundaries and saying no, and it makes me think of my own challenges around that.

I think about my fears around rejection. Not only am I afraid of hearing NO, I'm also afraid of saying it, and both are for the same reasons: they make me feel unliked and not accepted. We all want to be liked, so we adjust our behaviors. We're extra polite to strangers, we stand in line, we say yes when we want to say no, and we wear pants when out in public.[*]

We accommodate others to keep them happy, especially people we have relationships with. This desire to be liked and accepted can be more of a need, as it taps into our primal need to survive.

---

[*]   C'mon, you know you wouldn't if you could get away with it.

For thousands of years, we humans had to live, eat, sleep, travel, and hunt in groups in order to increase our chances for survival. Being in a group was necessary to stay alive, so gaining acceptance from the group was literally a matter of life and death. We've been doing this for so long that it's been baked into our wiring, so even though it may no longer be a matter of survival, we still work ridiculously hard to stay "in" and avoid rejection, because **feeling left out and rejected brings up those ancient anxieties of danger.**

If you're reading this book, you're most likely not part of a group where rejection means you're ostracized and banished into the jungle, where you'll surely get eaten by a hippopotamus,[*] but the pain and stress of being disliked and rejected are still the same. Survival for us is less physical and more psychosocial now, and although we can avoid hungry hungry hippos, we still suffer damage socially and emotionally. So we'll still chase approval and acceptance from others, thinking it's love, because our need for it is so visceral. Not only do our choices revolve around needing acceptance and avoiding rejection—we also make choices to avoid the potential for rejection. This means we don't put ourselves out there as much, take as many risks, speak our truths, or simply say NO to people.

Being left out or rejected signals feelings like we're not going to survive. This is why FOMO feels so trashy, and why you're not lying when you tell someone you love "I can't live without you," because it really feels like that.[**]

We are motivated to be connected, and too heavily motivated to keep our relationships intact, even if those relationships aren't healthy. The kicker is, we most often do this without even realizing it; it's literally what makes us human. Chasing validation subconsciously kept us alive for thousands of years, but now as the small villages have been replaced with big cities and communities with

---

[*]   Okay, fine, hippos don't eat people, but they will kill us if we let our guard down.
[**]   SPOILER ALERT: You CAN live without them, but that deathly feeling of losing someone is still real, and I'm not here to minimize it.

Internet strangers, **trying to keep everyone happy is going to be the death of us.**

I know it's painful when people don't like us, but we have to recognize that now, there's just too many people to try and win over. Gone are the days of us living in small villages and communities, and hello to cities of millions and an online world that feels unlimited. We can now count likes and read opinions about ourselves from people we've never met, and the deeper we dive into these worlds, the more that dread of rejection pays us a visit.

We can't make everybody happy; there are way too many people. It's okay that we want to, because that's how we were wired to be, but if the realization of genuine love is important, we're going to have to do the work to break the cycle, and the first step in the work is understanding why we care so much in the first place.

The more we can establish self-love and see ourselves as a source of love, the less we'll be running around, thinking we're chasing a wonderful feeling, when really we're just running away from a dreadful one.

So let's cut ourselves some slack for caring what other people think and wanting their approval, but know that if we can work beyond those feelings, there's a whole new life, and a whole lot more love to be realized.

Rejection is no longer a death sentence, and there will always be someone who just doesn't like you.

Love for self includes saying no to others and being okay with parts of you that others may not approve of.

TRYING TO KEEP EVERYONE HAPPY IS GOING TO BE THE DEATH OF US.

10.

YOU CAN ONLY HAVE UNCONDITIONAL LOVE FOR . . .

The chase for unconditional love is a strong force that makes us do many foolish things. We got this idea that love was supposed to be unconditional, and as real life slaps those possibilities out of us, instead of gaining a sense of realism and pragmatism, we double down on our search for the elusive love that exists without conditions.

Someone* told us the romantic idea that we can be loved without conditions, but then the first time our flawed family, friends, and others showed us that there were conditions to their love, we began looking elsewhere. Maybe we need to be more beautiful, and then people would love us unconditionally.** Maybe we need to be more famous, more successful, more accomplished, wealthier. The list goes on, but it becomes a driving force, almost an ultimate WHY to the choices we make in our life.

---

*   Probably the media and religion
**   Even though we fail to realize that beauty itself is the condition

The truth is that no matter how many people know you exist, the same percentage of them will love you. The comment section of my work is usually 95 percent love, 3 percent hate, and 2 percent trying to sell foreign exchange trading tips. It doesn't matter if I have 100 people in my life or 1,000,000. What we fail to remember is that 3 percent of hate from the 1,000,000 is 30,000 people and that can feel like a lot, enough to drown out the 950,000 ones that show love.[*] Everyone won't love us, and even if 100 percent of the people we met actually did, we would then begin to question what's wrong with them for loving such a klutz like us.[**]

If you're still reading despite my unnecessary math, then that's the most love I'm going to get from you, but I'm sure if I added a few more paragraphs with equations and charts, I would have lost you, and that's okay. Receiving unconditional love is a pipe dream; accessing it, on the other hand, is completely possible.

We can have unconditional love for love itself. We can place faith in love unconditionally, knowing that even when things don't work out our way, we won't abandon our ability to tap into love. **No one can take away our ability to love, it can only be forfeited.** When we realize we're capable of unconditional love, we can spend more time tapping inward into that instead of seeking it from others.

Love is so encompassing that it can love everything, even things we don't think are worthy of love.[***] I don't have to depend on fairy tales to believe in the power of love, I just have to go into my memories of the times I loved the most. I don't have to expect others to always love me, because I don't always love me, but I always have love for loving.

---

[*]   Not to mention the 20,000 teaching me when to sell the U.S. dollar for the euro
[**]   The irony of wanting unconditional love from others is that we can't receive it, because we don't have unconditional love for ourselves.
[***]   i.e., us at our "worst"

We need checks and balances from others to help adapt and evolve our behavior. It's okay for a one-year-old to play with their food and scream and cry in public, but less so for a teenager. Social approval and disapproval are valuable tools to keep us in line and grow. As an artist I encourage others not to become trapped in the prisons of others' opinions, especially in areas where we've discovered our exceptionalities, but that doesn't mean I don't value social contracts for the other parts of life.

Instead of hoping others would love us unconditionally, let's instead focus on better tools to connect and communicate with each other, so we can figure out each other's expectations, intentions, pet peeves, and enthusiasms. I want to be loved for who I am, but that still requires me to know who I am and to do a good job of explaining that to others, not simply expecting them to love what's in front of them at all times without exception.

It's okay that unconditional love doesn't exist between us, it really is. We can save ourselves years of looking for affection in the wrong places simply because of the broken belief that there can be more. **There definitely can be more love, but that love doesn't come to us from others, it comes from us.**

NO ONE CAN TAKE AWAY OUR ABILITY TO LOVE, IT CAN ONLY BE FORFEITED.

11.
LOVE THE VERB >
LOVE THE NOUN

When we think about love, when we long for love, what are we thinking about? Are we thinking about the experience and feelings that come from love, or are we thinking about the opportunities to love others? At this point you might say both, and at that point I'd want to call you a liar, but more important is that the question raises an idea that deserves our attention.

If we want more love, let's focus on the actions rather than the feelings. We all want to feel loved and experience all the beauty that comes with it. That desire may be the reason you picked up this book. The desire to experience love puts us in a mindset of figuring out how to receive more, as if love was only this thing that existed outside of us, so we have to search for it like treasure hunters. This can be true to some extent, but with a shift in mindset, we can focus more on the *act* of loving, and then we can tap into an endless source of love—ourselves. Love is more of an action than anything else, and it requires regular, deliberate, and sustained effort.

It's not that we need to find more love, we just need to experience more love. We have the power to create pathways to love both within and around us. Rather than chasing love in all other directions, let's tap into our own source.*

---
* Notice I said simpler, not easier.

This requires work, because instead of chasing love, we're now acting with love, allowing love to guide our choices instead of love being the desire behind them.

If you want more love in your life, then start loving more. The act of love is what's going to open us up to the feelings of love. We can't control how much love we receive or experience from others, but we can completely control how much love we share and send out into the world.

This may require us to let go of old ideas like love requires reciprocity. We treat love like a transaction—*give me some, and I'll give you some*—when really we should see it as *I share love because I enjoy sharing*. When we start to love others, we feel that love too, whether they reciprocate or not. Think about a baby: they don't do anything to love you back, they just exist.[*] We don't require babies to love us back, we just want to pour more and more love into them, and that act of pouring allows us to feel the flow of love as well.

We all know how to love selflessly, and that happens when we choose to focus on love the action, instead of the feeling. We put love into our projects, love into our families, love into adding 35 extra pillows when making our bed.[**] There's a satisfaction that comes from loving, and the less expectations we hold about receiving, the more we'll be able to feel the love that we're sharing.

We can chase attention, admiration, and validation forever, and all of that will feel like love for a bit, but nothing is going to replace the beautiful feeling of love coming from within. We are the source of love, the deepest well imaginable. Honoring this idea will have us spending less time trying to be loved and more time actually being LOVE.

---

[*]   And drool, and poop, and cry, and get their little fingers tangled in your beard, ripping out a patch that may never grow back.

[**]   Why is that a thing?

IF YOU WANT MORE LOVE IN YOUR LIFE, THEN START LOVING MORE.

NAZR:
A *love* STORY

"Buy property, one of those condos that they haven't started building yet." That's my mother's response when I hand her my latest check for my book deal.

After almost 10 years of living back at home, having little to show for my work, things were paying off. I was getting opportunities to perform on bigger stages, I was making major media appearances, and my public profile was growing.

Every time one of those awesome things happened for me I'd tell my mother, and her response was the same: "But are you making any money?"

She told me I'd had my fun, and I should go back to teaching. But now, I was standing in front of her in the kitchen, telling her I had a contract, with real money, and other promising opportunities to earn more. I had no intention of buying anything expensive, or showing off to anyone else, but my parents needed to see that I finally had something to show for all that work, enough zeroes to last me a few years.

And without losing a step, she replied, "Buy a property, prices are going up."

"Mom, this is called intellectual property, the prices of my work are going up too."

"I don't understand what you're going to do with all this money, you don't have a wife or kids or any family."

I'd waited a decade to make it this far, and as soon as I got there, she found ways to show me I hadn't gone far enough.

"Gimme some credit, I'm figuring this out. The people at the store gave you a discount because they recognized you as my mom, you just gave the lady at the bank a signed copy of my book. You have to admit, I did good, there's nothing wrong with saying you're proud of me."

I was spelling it out for her. I had trained myself not to need her approval this whole journey, but who am I kidding? We all want to know our parents are proud of us. No one else is going to know how much money I make, I'm only showing them, and as much as it is to dampen their worries that I'll go crazy and broke one day, it's also to prove their doubts wrong. Prove that I made something of myself, that I became one of the rare artists who actually figured out how to earn a living doing this. I knew I wasn't going to hear a "Good job" or a "You're right, you did it," but maybe I didn't deserve to be reminded of what else I didn't have.

"I won't say I'm proud of you, I made that mistake before and I got punished," she said, turning away.

"What?" I said. I had no idea what she was talking about. How had this conversation suddenly become about her?

"When we moved here, I was so proud of the job I got at the Kellogg's factory around the corner. I let it go to my ego, and then within two years God punished me and took it away. Then when your sister got married, I was so proud of my new son-in-law, so God punished me by breaking them up. I won't be proud of you, because I don't want God to punish me again and take it all away."

I didn't expect to hear that.

All this time I thought I couldn't do a thing to make my mom proud, never realizing that pride was the one thing she was avoiding with everything she had. She never told me she was proud of me, not out of malice, or some unrealistic immigrant parent expectations; she was doing so to protect me, out of love.

I understand now my mother's desire to avoid causing *nazr*—or "jinxing"—toward my success. I don't hold her beliefs in karma, but I get how she used it to console herself and to justify or explain the painful losses in her life. She got hurt on the job at the Kellogg's factory and that location eventually shut down a few years after, but that was not her fault. And my sister's marriage ending had nothing to do with my mom either. But deep down, she had been carrying that guilt inside her this whole time.

We create expectations for what love should look and feel like, but those expectations are only the size of our experiences. Although my mother wasn't helping to meet my need for validation, she was trying to keep me safe from divine powers she strongly believes in without me even knowing. It's not my place to argue about those beliefs, but instead just to recognize the love that motivates her actions. The older we get, the picture we had of our parents in childhood changes and gets complicated. They become more human, flawed, and vulnerable, but also the true scope of the effort they made for us, within the limits of what they know, becomes so much more pronounced.

There will always be a gap of understanding between ourselves and our parents, and often we put it on them to understand us. In some ways that makes sense: they've been around longer than us, they've been our age, we haven't been theirs. But love works both ways, and it's on everyone involved to bridge that gap. For me that means less about chasing things like validation from a parent who will always prioritize my well-being and that means not showing her checks and tempting her to have moments of pride, which terrify her into an encounter with karma-police-brutality.

For her, it could be letting me know she's on my team, and maybe she was already doing that as much as she could with the tools she had. Telling me to buy property was her way of expressing her wanting my safety and security. Telling me to get married and have ugly, smelly kids was her way of wanting me to experience a life richer than what I was experiencing alone, a deeper level of happiness.

Love can be the intention behind even some of the least heart-warming gestures.

Even if my mother doesn't understand what I'm doing, she doesn't want to do anything for me to lose it, even if that means depriving me of some short-term gratification for my tiny ego-toddler.

That's probably the exact type of love I need.

LONELY DANCES:
A *love* STORY

The first time we met was to watch the sun set and we hung out almost until the sun rose. My allergies were kicking in, and I was wiping my eyes with paper towels the whole time; little pieces of the tissue got caught in my beard. She touched my face to pick them out and it felt nice.

The next time we hung out, she spoke to me about what she observed from me, and she was spot-on. She mentioned that she sensed an unease from me about the life I had, and my need to take things deeper. She pointed out that I fidgeted a lot, and she looked at that as proof that I wanted to live a bigger life.

I'm not sure I ever felt seen by someone so quickly, so accurately; it felt nice. We ended the night kissing, and she pulled back, saying, "Slow and steady."

Weeks went by before I saw her again. She canceled a few times but apologized and acknowledged how annoying last-minute changes of plans are. She said we could go for a quick walk, and that turned into a long picnic. We exchanged a few more kisses.

A few days later I got a text from her that read: "Being intimate and in a relationship isn't something I'm open to, but we can still enjoy sunsets." Afraid she was completely brushing me off, I replied back, letting her know I respected her wishes but still wanted a conversation. She said we could chat the following week. When the following week arrived, I followed up, only to have her say, "This week isn't good, let's try next week."

Frustrated, I replied with a less than direct message pretty much saying, "Don't worry about it."

A few days later I called.

Me: Can't believe you picked up with your busy schedule.

Her: If I didn't want to pick up, I wouldn't have picked up. I'm not avoiding you; I just had a crazy week.

Me: A week so crazy you couldn't find eight minutes to talk to me?

Her: It would have been more than eight minutes, and I would have absorbed everything you said and needed time with it after. As the person most responsible for taking care of me, I have to do what's best.

Me (stubbornly): It would have taken less than eight minutes, and it still sucks that I have to reach out to you to find out that you plan on canceling on me.

Her: Honestly, I apologize if this hurts you, but I haven't been thinking about you. I've been busy with other parts of my life. That's why I told you I would need another week.

Me: I've just been experiencing this a lot from people. I don't understand how hard it is to stick to something you say you'll do.

Her: I don't hold it against people if they cancel on me, even if it's because they found better plans. I don't think it's useful to have those types of expectations on them.

Me: It's not just about expectations, it's about having . . . Don't you ever look forward to things?

Her: Yes.

Me: Like what?

She takes time to think before she replies.

Her: I look forward to my alone time.

Me: Well that explains a lot and honestly, I admire that. So if you like being alone, then the choices you're making will probably keep you isolated from others, then you're good. I'm not here to change what matters to you.

Her: Don't get me wrong, I still get lonely.

Me: Aha! Then why do you do things like this? What are you going to do when you feel lonely if you keep putting people like me on the back burner? *The only antidote to loneliness is connecti—*

Her: I dance.

Me: What?

Her: I dance, I dance around my apartment, I move and feel myself and connect with myself. That's how I cure my loneliness.

Me: Oh.

Her: **I think this is less about me, and more about your loneliness.** You should dance more.

Me: I should dance more.

We ended up speaking for another hour before we got off the phone. I'm not sure I was ready for her precision of clarity; it stung, but in a good way.

I never heard from her again, nor did I decide to ever reach out.

Although it wasn't in my favor, she was clear about her boundaries and honored them well, even at the risk of seeming like a villain in my eyes. That type of love toward herself created a connection far deeper than my company could ever compete with. She celebrated her own company by dancing.

We should all dance more, choosing the most important dance partner we can have: ourselves.

12.

OUR ADDICTION TO APPROVAL DENIES US LOVE

Hi, my name is Humble, and I'm an approval addict.

I've been sober for zero days. My addiction has taken over my life, ruined re-lationships, cost me financially, and had a negative impact on my health and self-worth.

I have trouble recognizing and accepting myself, and because of that I crave validation and attention from everyone else. This may have roots in parents who didn't have the tools to be there for me emotionally and in the intense experiences of racism I had growing up.

I say yes when I mean no.

I'm overly concerned with what others think about me.

I need my family and friends to accept and support my dreams before I can.

I want to work hard and be successful so I can prove all my doubters wrong. My doubters are anyone who rejected me in any way in the past; they need to regret it.

I wish I could be myself around everyone, but it's just not realistic. If people knew the real me, they wouldn't accept me.

I judge everyone else and put them down to make myself feel better.

I wish others felt sorry for me for all the things I've gone through.

I'm here to admit I have a problem and seek help.

It's reasonable that we all want some level of validation. We all need to be recognized and accepted by others on some level; it's a part of our interdependence. But when we don't get it from others, we should be able to provide it for ourselves. When our acceptance and recognition of ourselves isn't valued or possible, then we seek ongoing validation from others.

That endless chase for external validation reduces our ability to experience self-love.

My addiction to approval isn't a disease, or a character flaw, but it is a brain-wiring response to early developmental trauma caused by neglect. As I said earlier, that neglect wasn't intentional, my parents were in survival mode; they had moved to a new country and had to build a life. Feeding our tummies was the priority over nourishing us emotionally. Even if they had had all the time and money in the world, it's not like any of us automatically know how to be emotionally available to nourish others. I recognize the neglect but blame no one, and at this point, it's only my responsibility to make things better.

Approval is a salty potato chip—once you have one, you'll want more. None of us are weak for wanting it, but once we recognize the addiction, it's on us to do something about it.

Approval from others will never be as nutritious as our approval of ourselves. That's why self-respect is more important than self-esteem. Self-respect comes from not only recognizing and validating ourselves, but also from making tough choices that warrant that recognition and validation. That could be as simple as setting goals and doing the boring, repetitive, and often difficult work to achieve them.

I'll experience more love from sitting in a tub of ice, waking up at the same time every day, choosing journaling over looking at my phone, and stretching than I will receiving any type of attention or approval from anyone else. That's because these tough activities promote attention and approval toward myself, building my self-respect, which will always be a stronger foundation than my self-esteem.

But it doesn't have to be this way.

We can do the work one step at a time, and that first step is being willing to admit that we have an addiction.

> *"The opposite of addiction is not*
> *sobriety, it's connection."*
> — Johann Hari

We can beat this addiction by connecting with ourselves.

I will beat this addiction by creating a stronger connection with myself.

APPROVAL IS A SALTY POTATO CHIP —
ONCE YOU HAVE ONE, YOU'LL WANT MORE.

13.

HOW TO PUT YOURSELF FIRST WITHOUT BEING SELFISH

Saying no to people is hard. I still struggle with it, especially with people who won't take no for an answer. It could be a favor, or a social obligation, or wanting me to help them move.[*] It feels easier to say yes to them than justifying why you don't want to. Because let's be honest, saying "I don't want to" rarely feels like an option.

The challenge here is when you realize that saying yes to something means saying no to something else, probably something else that matters more to you.

Of all the love we seek to experience, it's the love for self that will have the biggest impact on our lives. It'll decide how much love we receive from others, and how well we treat ourselves. That process of self-love is based on the ever-improving relationship we have with ourselves; that means **we have to make ourselves a priority, just like any other important relationship we have.**

---

[*]   If you're over 30, don't ask your friends to help you move, someone's gonna get hurt.

So often we put the needs of others before our own because we don't want to look selfish or have the other person like us any less. What ends up happening is we become martyrs who think there's some sort of honor that comes from putting others before ourselves, even when it's one-sided. The truth is, there's no honor in it, it's romanticizing people-pleasing and another way to chase validation. It's not sustainable if our needs are continually unmet because we're too busy being there for others. Resentment and self-pity are sure to follow, and both of those are shrinking pathways to love.

The lack of "selfishness" we're displaying is really just making us ineffective people. It makes us less useful and valuable to ourselves and those we care about. We can't help others if we don't help ourselves. **Ignoring our own needs will make it harder to be there for those that matter most.** That will damage our relationship with ourselves, blocking the flow of love and further creating a dependency on the approval of others.

I'm not encouraging you to say, "Screw everyone else." I'm saying, in order to discover more self-love and to actually have juice in our battery to be there for others, we have to put our needs first, because the most important community we're a part of is the community of ourselves. That community consists of us in the present and every future version of ourselves.[*]

We need to make more decisions that take our future selves into consideration.

How will skipping the gym to rediscuss Debby's latest of 13 breakups in her on-again, off-again relationship impact me in five hours, five days, and five years?

Those three versions of you matter, as well as every other subsequent future version of you. It's the reason you wash those dishes before going to bed, because you don't want to leave the mess for the future you to deal with.[**]

---

[*] You now, you three hours from now, you tomorrow, you next week, you in five years—that's the community.

[**] Unless, of course, you're Homer Simpson and deferring responsibility to "future me" is your favorite pastime.

I completely understand why it's easier to be there for others than it is to be there for ourselves. What other people think of us matters, especially when we don't have a strong relationship with ourselves. Also, we're not as clear with our own needs compared to what others ask of us. They know what they want, while we kinda think we maybe know what's important.

If we're not clear with our needs, we'll always be saying "yes" to everyone else's demands. That's because we haven't taken the time to figure out if they match up or get in the way of our own needs. The reason we haven't been clear with our needs is because we're scared. Being vague is a language of fear; we're scared we won't hit our mark, so we don't bother choosing something to aim at to begin with. What we fail to acknowledge is that we can't hit a mark we don't aim for. Making any decision from fear is taking us away from love. To have a better relationship with ourselves and further open pathways of love in our lives, we have to make the time and be clear on what we want from life.

The more detailed, the better.

I have to be clear with my loved ones that I can't spend more than two to three hours with them because then I may get overwhelmed and become a grouchy beard. I may not be able to go into detail to explain that as a creative, I have to protect my peace and my mental wealth through doing the things I need to do for myself. If I don't feel good, I'm not of any value to anyone else. That may mean leaving the party early, or not attending the party at all. Just like you, I'm afraid of disappointing others; but **I, like you, am slowly realizing that it doesn't matter what others think about me if I don't like myself.**

So to further love myself, I have to identify my needs as clearly as possible and put them first. Through doing so, I begin to feel better and need other people's validation much less.

Our relationships are the most important things we have in this human experience. Our relationship with ourselves is the most important one of them all. Without a strong relationship with ourselves, we're limiting our ability to have growing relationships with others. The selfishness we should avoid is not one where we put ourselves first. **Real toxic selfishness is expecting others to put us first.** Anyone that expects you to put their needs before yours is the one being selfish, and you have to get to a point where you love yourself enough not to bend to those demands.

"No" is a complete sentence.

Be that best friend to yourself and put your needs first, and make sure those needs are clear and can be shared with everyone. The more you stand up for yourself, the less others can and will try to run you over. The more your own needs are met, the more you'll be able to help others meet theirs.

IF WE'RE NOT CLEAR WITH OUR NEEDS, WE'LL ALWAYS BE SAYING "YES" TO EVERYONE ELSE'S DEMANDS.

14.

LOVE IS NOT IMPRESSING OTHERS, IT'S IMPRESSING OURSELVES

There are major life milestones that we think we have to hit to stay in everyone else's favor. That could include finishing college, getting a good job, finding an acceptable partner, having a certain body-fat percentage or clear skin. It's an endless list we try to go through in hopes that getting enough things checked off will make us deserving of love.

I thought making some money as an artist would do it for me. Very few people believed that I could do it, and although they didn't outright dump on my goals, they would speak passive-aggressively about them.[*] The tone of their voice would be a bit higher pitched, and they'd throw around words like "realistic" and ask if I was sure this was what I wanted to do. They would bring up other people who had since married, had kids, and now owned a house, all while I was still couch surfing in my 30s. I thought if I made enough money, then it

---

[*]   I am Canadian, after all.

would prove to them that I was worthy of their support and love. I literally started showing checks to my parents as I got them, but that didn't make me feel better. Maybe I needed to make more money, or have a bestseller, or get some major press coverage for my work.

Then all of that happened: I got another big check, I debuted at number seven on the bestsellers list, and I was on some major podcasts like *The Breakfast Club*.[*] The euphoria of ticking off the boxes was short-lived. There was a voice in my head that kept saying, *You need to debut at number one, then they'll really respect you.* Nothing was ever enough to make that voice happy.

What I slowly realized was that there's too many people to try to impress, and instead of trying to impress them all, I had to take the idea of impressing them off my list; the only person worth impressing . . . is myself. Doing amazing things that excite others isn't the prerequisite to feeling love, it's actually shrinking the pathways of love we have. Even impressing myself may not lead to loving myself if it creates an expectation that I have to accomplish or win something all the time. The people in our lives that we love don't have to constantly impress us to earn our love, we love them regardless, and that can also apply to loving ourselves.

Now you may be reading this in your bathrobe with nacho chip crumbs scattered in your beard, wondering how anyone could love such a sloth, and with that I agree: it would be hard. So let's find a healthy middle ground between killing ourselves to accomplish a bunch of things and doing absolutely nothing; that middle ground is focusing on our *efforts instead of the outcomes.* These efforts aren't for others, they're for us.

Impress yourself with the effort you put into your life, and the rest you take to enhance those efforts. I'm writing this at 8:48 A.M. on a Friday morning, fresh from a good night's sleep. Only a few months ago, I

---

[*]   Which was a personal dream of mine

was falling asleep at 7:30 A.M. and waking up around 2:00 P.M., trying to figure out how to salvage my day, all while picking nacho chips out of my beard for breakfast. It feels great knowing I'm adding another brick to the castle of my book and doing it early enough that I can spend the day working on other things that excite me and hanging out with people that make me feel great. **Loving myself isn't always the reward for doing the work, it's getting my ass up early enough to do that work, even when I'm not in the mood.**

More than half of what I write never makes the final pages and won't have a chance to validate me. We often mistake validation for love, and because of that, leaving work on the cutting room floor feels like waste. But if I write because I love writing, and I'm proud of myself for the consistent effort, then the simple act of writing is widening the pathways for love to flow. I'm impressed with myself not for an accomplishment, but for simply trying. I only have control over my effort, and knowing I used that effort to the best I can is what widens my ability to experience more love. It's not about doing or being enough; there is no "enoughness" to experience love, just movement in life to keep it flowing.

How can you impress yourself more so you spend less time chasing admiration and acceptance from others?

Maybe the only milestones we need to hit are checking off days where we gave it all we had.

THE PEOPLE IN OUR LIVES
THAT WE LOVE DON'T
HAVE TO CONSTANTLY
IMPRESS US TO EARN
OUR LOVE, WE LOVE THEM
REGARDLESS, AND THAT
CAN ALSO APPLY TO
LOVING OURSELVES.

15.

LOVING YOURSELF IS BEING YOUR OWN BEST FRIEND

I can be a great friend to others and horrible to myself. I live with myself, and I'm sick of my shit. I'm sick of my excuses, my flaws, and my inconsistencies. I'm well aware of how I can be difficult to live with. Like you, I still feel like other people have it together much more than I do. I admire people who I want to be like, and most of them are rarely like me. They seem more confident, nicer, more organized, and easier to be around. Because of this, I'll put their needs before mine, think before I say things to them, make room for them to have bad moments, and try to help them in any way I can.

I can be a great friend to them, and I started to wonder what would happen if I was a better friend to myself.

We all treat others better than we treat ourselves. We take care of our loved ones more than we take care of ourselves, and that's because we really love them. To really love ourselves isn't an act only available to people who meditate in the woods or do intermittent fasting, it's simply treating ourselves the way we treat those we love, no mystery about it.

Self-love is being our own best friend.

We all know how to be good friends; it comes naturally when we're around people we like. We want them to be right, we want them to win, we want to support them in their growth, but then when it comes to ourselves, we think we have to earn the right to get that same treatment. With our loved ones, we don't question whether they're worthy of our love, and rarely do they actually do things to make that love fade away. So let's take that same idea and apply it to ourselves.

Let's be our own best friend.

Let's be accepting of ourselves despite our flaws with minimal judgment. Let's be our biggest cheerleader. Let's praise ourselves, laugh at ourselves, honor our needs, and spend time with ourselves. Let's have fun with ourselves. Like a real best friend, let's listen to, trust, and forgive ourselves. Let's figure out what's required to support ourselves and grant it.

When we go through shit, let's ask, *What would I do if I was supporting a friend in this situation?* Sometimes the answer is going to be giving a shoulder to cry on, lending an ear or a journal to vent to, or giving a safe place to be distracted. Sometimes it'll be acting as an advocate for your side of the story. Other times it'll be calling yourself out on your bullshit. Many of the things real friends do for us are things we can also receive from ourselves.

Of course, this is much more challenging than it sounds. It's easier to be a friend to others than it is to befriend ourselves, but heading in that direction with the intention of strengthening self-friendship will do wonders for experiencing more love.

> ### *"Get high off your own supply . . . of love"*
> ### — Humble The Poet*

---

* This deserves to be a quote on a corny mountainous background hung in classrooms and cubicles everywhere.

My goal is to take the mystery out of love, and help you redirect your best practices inward. We can really be the support we long for from others, and by doing so, we'll compromise ourselves much less to chase outside validation and approval. There's no one-size-fits-all recipe for self-love, just as there's no one-size-fits-all for a best friend.

Sometimes self-love is yelling at yourself to get out of bed, and other times it'll be gently telling yourself to get a few extra hours of sleep because your body needs the rest. **None of us are perfect friends, and none of our friends are perfect, but we can still love them and ourselves just the same.**

A best friend lets you know when you're being a dumbass, they let you know that you're better than a person who would stay in that unhealthy relationship. A best friend is someone you get in trouble with, and who bails you out if things get too sticky. We can be all of these things to ourselves.

We don't constantly question whether our friends are worthy of our love, and their mistakes don't make them any less wonderful, they just become lovable dummies. We can see ourselves as lovable dummies as well, and we can start immediately by doing all the things a great friend would do for us, but for ourselves.

You deserve to be your friend, and you deserve the love that comes from that. Even if you don't have a lot of friends, you can still imagine what great friendship looks and feels like, and direct that energy your way.

So the next time you're feeling down, take a breath and ask, *What would my best friend do?*[*] There's no wrong answer, the spirit and effort of being your own best friend will yield an abundance of love, both for yourself and for others to share in.

---

[*]   #WWMBFD, let's make that a thing.

SELF-LOVE IS BEING OUR OWN BEST FRIEND.

16.

LOVE IS FORGIVING YOURSELF

We can't experience much love if forgiveness isn't invited to the party. We all want forgiveness, but it's hard to give it, and often the hardest times to forgive are the times it needs to happen the most.

Forgiveness has to be voluntary; it's being open to going on a journey to change how we feel and our attitudes toward something bad that's happened. That means allowing negative emotions like resentment and vengeance to pass so we can move forward.

The misunderstanding around forgiveness is that we're okay with the bad things that happened, and to forgive is to accept those things. The truth is, forgiveness has little to do with what happened, and much more to do with our need to move forward without carrying these heavy burdens of emotions with us.

Forgiveness is a dialect of love. "I forgive you" translates to "I love myself enough to no longer hold on to this." So when we don't forgive ourselves, we deny ourselves love. We may purposely deny expressing love through forgiveness because deep down, we feel like we don't deserve it since we do bad things, some of which seem unforgivable, but that's not true. We've proven the power of forgiveness when we forgive those we love, and as a practice of loving ourselves, we have to forgive ourselves as well.

We're really good at blaming ourselves for things, even things that are out of our control. We allow these moments to define us. We'll all make stupid choices that lead to stupid outcomes; that doesn't make us stupid people. Making a horrible decision doesn't make us a horrible person, and part of recognizing that is forgiving ourselves for the things we do.

The opposite of forgiveness is resentment, and resentment is a barrier to love.

The opposite of forgiveness is punishment, and punishment rarely occupies space with love.

Not forgiving encourages victimhood, another mindset that blocks pathways of love.

Love flows and requires movement, and forgiveness inspires things to keep moving. **Forgiveness isn't saying everything is cool, it's saying that the uncool things aren't worth holding on to** moving forward.

When we make space to forgive ourselves, we also create space to forgive others. That's important to reducing the blockages love faces in our lives. Forgiving ourselves also reduces the need to receive forgiveness from others. Others may not be ready to forgive us, they may not have all the facts, or they may just be in too much pain to forgive, but none of that should stop us from moving forward with the limited time we have in our lives.

It is important to take that weight off your chest, reduce the blockages, and allow the love that flows within you to move more freely. Here are some practical ideas to help encourage more forgiveness toward yourself and others:

1. Make Space for the Shitty Feelings

Sometimes when we fight feelings, we feed them. We have to face the discomfort and make space and time to feel the things we feel. If we need forgiveness we'll probably feel ashamed, guilty, regretful, disgusted with ourselves, among a gang of other unpleasant emotions that come. Let go and feel them, cry them out, write them out, scream them out; no longer will they be pent up, serving as a dam that blocks the paths of love that should be moving all around you.

2. Forgive Yourself Tangibly

Kamal Ravikant says to write it all down, and then throw it in the ocean. I recently wrote down something I needed forgiveness for, put the pages in a pot in my kitchen, and threw a match in. It felt cathartic.* It's not that the ocean waves or fire will take away the original sin—it's that we've taken it all off our chest, made our peace with it, and now have done something to let it go. If you don't live near the ocean or want to play with fire, then just throw it in the garbage, or a paper shredder, or use scissors. Maybe you didn't write anything down and you simply have to say aloud, "I forgive you." Maybe you have to scream it a few times. Maybe you seal the deal with a special forgiveness dance.** Whatever it is, the gesture of forgiveness has to leave your head and be something real; that's the way to ensure we get closer to the last step.

---

* And also nerve-racking in that at any moment the smoke detector might go off or I'd burn down my kitchen.
** Which, in my head, looks a lot like the chicken dance

3. Feel the Forgiveness (or at least imagine what it should feel like)

We've all forgiven and been forgiven, and we know what it should feel like. We should feel lighter and freer, letting out a big sigh of relief. It may not be completely liberating, but progress is all we should aim for, and if you feel better than you did before, then love has found more room to flow.

4. Celebrate the Lessons

When we mess up, we learn. That's something to celebrate. You made a mistake, you realized the mistake, you learned from it, and you'll do better. Write that down, say it out loud until it makes sense. Solidify the learning because that's the silver lining to all the mistakes we make.

Forgiveness is an essential tool of love, and to get better at it, we need to practice it as much as possible. When we don't forgive ourselves, we deem ourselves unworthy of love, and that's love in our lives we could share with others and the world. Repeat those steps as often as needed, make a routine of it. Just don't fall in the ocean or burn down your house.

FORGIVENESS ISN'T
SAYING EVERYTHING
IS COOL, IT'S SAYING
THAT THE UNCOOL
THINGS AREN'T WORTH
HOLDING ON TO.

17.

SELF-LOVE MEANS KNOWING WHAT MATTERS

When I go on social media, I almost instantly start feeling worse about myself. This is often because I look at what other people have and what they're doing, and it makes me feel like I don't have enough, or I'm not doing enough in my own life. These gaps we start to identify in our lives are amplified on social media, because it's an endless source of people living a "for display purposes only" life, designed to make us feel like less.

Maybe it's seeing a couple celebrate a pregnancy, or a proposal, or buying a house. These moments are worth celebrating, but they have the rest of us questioning ourselves and then beating up on ourselves for not being there as well.

What we have to remember is that this comparison game is never ending, and we always lose. There will always be someone doing or having something we don't. Instead of trying to keep up with the Kardashians, we have to look inward and better define what actually matters to us. Knowing what we value helps us realize what we don't. **We should spend less time trying to check off things on someone else's bucket list, and instead spend more time figuring out what actually matters to us.**

Doing the work to know what we value means getting intimate, vulnerable, and honest with ourselves; that's the recipe for connection. When we can go deep inwardly, see what's really there, we'll quickly realize that what works for others may not really tickle our fancy.

I've always wanted to feel free. At first I thought freedom meant having tons of money, beyond simply being debt free and able to support myself, but I quickly realized that with every little bump in earnings I achieved, so did a little bump in my lifestyle. The next thing I knew, I was trapped in car payments and a slave to other expensive habits that then required me to stick with a job that was no longer keeping my fire lit. Over the years, I made adjustments to both how I earned and what I spent to find a better balance. Although I feel freer than before, more constraints in my life revealed themselves.

I now realize my most important freedoms are not from the world around me, but from what's happening inside. I'm not free if I'm still a slave to my desires, emotions, and impulses; no amount of passive income and being my own boss can help with that. Now when I scroll through the phone, I don't envy the person with the Lamborghini, I envy the one who takes cold showers and eats very little sugar, OR the one who's not even on social media to begin with.

Going inward and knowing our deep values sets us on a journey of self-awareness and discovery and strengthens the relationship we have with ourselves. It also becomes our yardstick to what we consider success, and that will reduce how often we're comparing ourselves to others.

Knowing our deepest values also adds clarity to the connections and relationships we make with others. Lining up our values is important when working with people, having friendships, and in romantic relationships. We don't know if someone's a good match for us if we haven't spent time figuring out what matters to us in the first place. Our deepest values mean more than the surface-level things we have in common. Sure, someone may have the same ethnicity and heritage as you, but what about their values when it comes to the more universal elements of being alive?

Here are some questions you can ask yourself to better understand your true values:

- What do you spend your time doing?
- Where do you spend *most* of your energy?
- After bills and expenses, what do you spend most of your money on?
- What do you visually consume on a day-to-day basis?
- What do you think about most?
- What do you envision most?
- Do you talk to yourself about positive or negative things?
- How do you talk to others?
- What goals do you set for yourself?
- Who inspires you?

There's going to be a pattern that emerges from answering these questions, and from those patterns, we'll learn two to three deep priorities that really matter beyond anything else.

Examples of core values:

- Hope
- Service
- Responsibility
- Faith
- Honor
- Trust

- Freedom
- Honesty
- Integrity
- Justice
- Truth

Often, I just ask myself, "Who do you admire, and why?" and realize that **a lot of my values are revealed in those people I look up to.** It helps pull me away from what everyone else thinks is important and lets me figure out what really matters to my core. Then I spend less time getting FOMO for places I didn't really want to go and envy for things I never really wanted.

When we know what matters to us, we also know what doesn't, and we can spend more time, energy, and focus in the right places. That stronger sense of self and clarity is important to keep the flow of love in our life, because we'll spend more time in gratitude, and less time in lack and desire.

So go on, ask yourself the important questions. Figure out what's really important, because within those things lies more experiences of love. Loving ourselves is knowing ourselves, and that journey is really endless when we take it inward. Knowing what matters to us will save us time, energy, attention, and effort, all better spent toward loving ourselves. You can then leave all the other stuff to the show-offs on social media.

WE SHOULD SPEND LESS
TIME TRYING TO CHECK
OFF THINGS ON SOMEONE
ELSE'S BUCKET LIST, AND
INSTEAD SPEND MORE
TIME FIGURING OUT WHAT
ACTUALLY MATTERS TO US.

18.
ENVY PULLS US AWAY FROM LOVE

I'm not sure I get to decide to envy somebody, it sort of just happens, but I can definitely make myself aware of that envy. Envy is simply coveting what someone else has, and it's not always a bad thing.

I envy Neil Pascricha's ability to write for three hours a day and consider it therapeutic.

I envy Charlamagne tha God's indiscriminate and selfless service to everyone he crosses paths with.

I envy Rupi Kaur's resolve to create, be authentic, and speak for what matters, even at the expense of her own career and safety.

I envy Dave Chappelle's honesty, timing, and freedom as a creative.

I envy Malcolm X's resolve.

I envy Lilly Singh's work ethic.

I envy couples who have successfully cohabitated for 50 years.

Envy can do a lot to help reveal what's really important to us. **If you want to know what matters to you, look at who you envy, and why.**

Envy isn't jealousy. Envy is yearning for what someone else has, while jealousy is the fear that something we have may be taken away by someone else. Jealousy is about control, which is the language of fear; envy is a bit more complicated.

There's more than one type of envy, and it's important to know when that envy is going to bring out some self-awareness and improvement, and also when it's going to bring us down a darker path, far away from love.

There's benign envy, that's just simply wishing you had what other people had, only focusing on the good. Maybe you wish you had Beyoncé's body, or Jay-Z's ability to still have hair in his 50s, or their combined fertility to have twins. Maybe you wish you had your sister's patience, or your best friend's work ethic, or your dad's ability to fall asleep anywhere, anytime. Benign envy helps to reveal what matters to us and doesn't really mean we have issues with the people who have the things we covet.

Then there's emulative envy, which, like benign envy, focuses on the good and holds the belief that the things we envy are attainable. This is why we may do our hair and makeup like our favorite celebrity, or wear shoes from our favorite athlete, or even just copy our older siblings. Emulative envy probably comes from our survival days, copying the best hunters and providers. This type of envy is still pretty harmless.

Then there's the malicious, insidious envy. This is the most painful and causes the most damage. This is when you love what another person has, but also hate that it's them who has it. This can be a co-worker getting a promotion, or a friend getting engaged, or watching a rival sports team have their championship parade. Sometimes we unconsciously assume they don't deserve what they have as the resentment deepens, and we start to have unpleasant thoughts that lead to *schadenfreude*, the idea that someone's misfortune brings you pleasure.

> *"The envious man thinks that if*
> *his neighbor breaks a leg, he will*
> *be able to walk better himself."*
> — Helmut Schoeck

This form of malicious envy is something we're all guilty of at different levels. It's pain that comes from the good fortune of others, even people we care about. This type of envy feeds resentment, in the company of which is one of the most unpleasant places we can find ourselves.

There's times when we can feel envious of the good fortune of our friends and family, even when it benefits us. This can relate to our upbringing. Many of us feel like we didn't get enough love, support, and attention from those who raised us and now we thirst for more as adults. A bronze medal can feel better than a silver medal, because squeezing out a spot on the podium feels better than losing out on the gold.

Seeing others allows us to see where we're constrained in life. When we envy someone else, we feel ashamed and embarrassed about it, so we bury it deep, not realizing that we're only making it worse.

There's only value to envy if we bring it to light, say it out loud, or write it in our book. There's nothing to be embarrassed about, the **envy is less about your relationship with that other person than it is about your relationship with yourself.** Pseudo-positive pep talks to yourself wishing them the best won't contribute as much to growth as admitting your envy exists.

Also understanding that going deeper into envy can also reduce its sting. Although Neil writes much more in a day than I do, we write about different things, and have different brains, and he's written many more books than me, which by default will have allowed him more time and experience in finding a better groove when it comes to being in front of the computer typing away.

Maybe your friend got engaged before you, but that doesn't mean you haven't been spending your time on other things that matter. The goal isn't to stop caring that they have things you want, it's to dial down the malicious and turn up the benign.

When we focus on the good parts of envy, realizing that someone else has what we want is proof that we can get it too. We can get bitter or get better by this understanding. We all want people in our lives that celebrate our good fortune, so let's start by being that for others. You can tell others you envy what they have or what they have accomplished and still be happy for them. **Bringing that envy into the light is a great way of keeping yourself from getting dark.**

So don't shame yourself for feeling envious, and don't resent the people you envy. Envy is an opportunity to learn about yourself, connect with what really matters, and practice celebrating others, all of which are important ways to further open the pathways of love through our lives.

IF YOU WANT TO KNOW WHAT MATTERS TO YOU, LOOK AT WHO YOU ENVY, AND WHY.

19.
LOVE YOUR FLAWS AND INCOMPLETENESS

I often imagine a day when I have abs and can post subtle thirst-trap photos disguised as happy accidents. The idea of six-pack abs has been a sordid history with me. I think I was in middle school and my high school–aged sister told me to start working out so I could have abs. Before that, I hadn't noticed the difference between my pudgy tummy and anyone else, but after that conversation, washboard stomachs stood out to me everywhere.

I have plenty of friends with these "ideal" body types, and none of them are particularly happier than me. None of them are devoid of insecurities, and very few of them have ever bragged about the benefits of looking like swimsuit models.

Love doesn't arrive when we're perfect, because if that was the case, love would never arrive. We are all flawed human beings, and we're supposed to be. Self-love is the practice of accepting our flaws and the things that make us incomplete, instead of trying to always remedy them.

I don't want to say you are already "enough," or that you're already "worthy" of love. Instead I want to say there's no such thing as enough and worthy in the first place; it's a made-up idea in an attempt to measure something that can't be measured—us.

It's okay to suck at things in our lives. **Everyone is an idiot in some department of their existence, including everyone we look up to, and that's fine; let's just be lovable idiots.** Everyone we love has flaws and we know that, but we love others who have flaws and moments of idiocy, so we can afford that same love toward ourselves.

We're supposed to make mistakes and stumble; accept failures as part of the journey. Let's be okay laughing at ourselves as well. No one is beyond being made fun of, and feeling like a goof sometimes is an essential part of trying to live a good life. Making fun of our own flaws is a great way to live with them. I have a crooked nose with one working nostril and Chiclets for front teeth and a cute tummy that makes me giggle when you poke it.

Let's see the pros of our "flaws." That means expressing gratitude, realizing that just because we think something doesn't mean that the thought is true. We live in a society of consumerism, so the mantra will always be "You're not good enough, spend money to be better." And we don't have to fall for that bullshit.

Let's be vulnerable and talk out loud about the things we're not the most secure about. Bringing them out reduces their sting and will connect us with others, who are definitely feeling the same.

Self-love isn't trying to fix ourselves, but accepting who we are. That doesn't mean we shouldn't take care of ourselves, but it does mean we need to abandon that limiting belief that we need to be more before we deserve love.

These old limiting beliefs haunt us, constructing an invisible prison we don't always realize we're trapped in. And even though these beliefs aren't based in truth, thinking them over and over builds the walls higher and higher as we manifest them.

Progress can come from simply exploring the question: "Who would I be if I didn't hold any insecurities?"

We limit ourselves because of these insecurities, not realizing that going beyond what's familiar can help us develop new connections that have yet to be realized within us. We have primal and opioid systems that will be triggered by new experiences that will only better us.

Although a bunch of abs are no longer on my list of goals, being healthier definitely is. I want to have more energy to do things in the day and live to see the day when more of my beard hairs are gray than black.

The list of things I'm not good at eclipses the tiny list of things I do well, and that's okay. I'm an ever-improving work of art, and although I do have a feeling of incompleteness—a hollow hole within me—I'm no longer trying to fill it with validation, attention, or even love. I'm accepting it for what it is, a pit of potential, knowing that the only moment I'll actually be complete is with the last breath I take. The hole is a part of us; it's what keeps us moving forward. The world will sell us things to try to fill that hole, but really, all we can do is accept it as a part of us, knowing our most fulfilling moments are just that, moments. They add texture and color, but they'll never completely fill in the blank space, and that's okay.

Accepting ourselves and opening up those pathways to love takes practice. We can't just say we accept ourselves, we have to get naked in front of the mirror and start celebrating what's in front of us. A beautiful body that's been with us since day one, a crooked smile that filled up others when they saw it, textured skin that people still love to hug, and a person who, despite not being completely symmetrical, is worthy of having and BEING all the beauty that exists in life.

PROGRESS CAN
COME FROM SIMPLY
EXPLORING THE
QUESTION: "WHO WOULD
I BE IF I DIDN'T HOLD
ANY INSECURITIES?"

20.

LOVING YOURSELF IS BEING YOUR OWN NURTURING PARENT

Let's keep it 1,000 percent. Many of our deepest desires of love come from our twisted relationships with our parents. Maybe we were three years old and then had a sibling, and all of a sudden the attention* we got was then directed toward the little squishy thing called your little sibling. We did anything and everything to earn that love from our parents. Some of us had super-toxic parents who should have never had kids, but many of us had relatively common upbringings with flawed individuals who tried their best, kept us alive, and did a semi-decent job of raising us.

We assume that along with their 50-hour work weeks, dealing with their own shit, and providing us with our basic necessities they also needed to have Danny Tanner and Uncle Phil moments with us, so we set our bars according to what we thought would earn their love, and headed for it. For some, it's a degree, a job, a spouse, and some kids; for others it's being the best at something. It could have also been displaying strength, not crying, not asking for help, or being self-sufficient so as not to seem disgusting and undesirable to those

---
* Which we thought was love

people who raised us and whose love we crave. We were kids, and our limited understanding of ourselves and the challenges of life meant we weren't aware of all that our parents were dealing with, and what they did for us. We wanted more, and subconsciously blamed ourselves when we didn't get it.

As we get older, we extend that need for attention from our parents to our lovers; mommy and daddy issues are real. We lean into what's familiar, and the first experiences of love we experienced were from our parents, regardless of how healthy it was. We then spend our time subconsciously re-creating that in our own way. Now there are no more siblings to compete with, we think we know better, but ultimately, we may be setting ourselves up for failure, trying to find this high level of love in the wrong place.

The truth is, none of our parents were ever going to give us the flawless, unconditional love we crave, and the journey to make up for that with other love-thirsty toddler-adults is going to leave us unfulfilled. Some of us evolve to a point where we recognize the unpleasant moments of our childhood are impacting our adulthood. This recognition can often come with finger-pointing and blame, so we need to evolve past that. I don't want to call it forgiving our parents, because we'll find ourselves dealing with many of the demons they dealt with, and that context is important. Realizing that adult life is pretty much the same as childhood (except it includes bills and back pain) can help us realize we may have expected too much of those who raised us. We wanted more love and more nurturing. We wanted a corny monologue at the end of the episode that makes it all better. We want our parents to have impeccable EQs, greet us at eye level, and read between the lines of our behavior. Those expectations move onto our future partners.[*] Neither our parents nor any other people in our life will live up to these expectations, but there is someone who can.

That person is us.

---

[*] "If you really loved me, you would know what to do."

Instead of searching outward for this perfect nurturing parent/lover, we can scratch that itch ourselves. When we place these expectations on ourselves, we'll quickly realize how little work we've done to understand ourselves. Do we always stop to ask why we have the emotional outbursts we have? Are we reading between the lines of our own words and choices? When we choose self-awareness in the spirit of loving and nurturing ourselves, we can really tap into the abundant love we seek from others.

There is no one more qualified to honor and articulate our needs and boundaries than us. We can speak to our inner ego-toddler lovingly with warmth at our lowest moments. We can even practice self-*havening,* which is the practice providing ourselves with additional safe space through hugging and caressing ourselves as we revisit traumatic moments in our lives. We can literally hug ourselves and feel better from it. We can set 10 minutes a day to write letters to ourselves the way we wish our perfect mom and dad could have. We can celebrate our magnificence the way we wish our parents did or held us during our lowest moments.

Loving ourselves is being the nurturing parents we're perpetually seeking in our lovers, our social media followers, and our mentors. We have the skills and the inside scoop on how we feel, and why we feel it. I don't have any kids,[*] but I'm pretty sure when we become real parents, we'll be far from perfect. That shouldn't be something to be afraid of; if anything, that'll feed compassion toward our parents, who mostly tried their best with the tools they had in the situations they were in, despite their own personal shit. We won't be perfect parents to our future kids, but we can be amazing parents to ourselves. When we foster that love, we'll seek it less from others, and instead have more to share and give.

Your self-nurturing parent can love you at your worst.

---

[*]   I think?

Your self-nurturing parent will know when "I'm fine" isn't really "I'm fine."

Your self-nurturing parent can celebrate and love those sides of you that you don't even like about yourself.

Your self-nurturing parent can view your darkness without guilting and shaming you.

Your self-nurturing parent can be anything and everything you've ever wanted a life full of love to be. You can fake it until it becomes real—we all do that with others, it'll work with us as well.

The desire for a higher love is in all of us, and the not-so-secret secret is that it will only be satiated in the long term when it comes from within. Like any relationship, it's going to take a shit ton of work, and it's not going to be easy, but in those moments when you really connect with the scared, lonely, hurt child inside, it's going to feel amazing.

THERE IS NO ONE MORE QUALIFIED TO HONOR AND ARTICULATE OUR NEEDS AND BOUNDARIES THAN US.

21.

LOVE IS BREAKING OUR CYCLES

Some of the strategies I had to do to survive my childhood were things that ended up hurting me as an adult. I had to carry myself with an aura of aggression to avoid being picked on. I had to tiptoe around expressing my needs to my family because, as they were working immigrants just trying to pay the bills, it felt like their plates were full. I had to hide my feelings because that's what tough guys did.

As a child who was still developing, my needs should have been met, I should have felt safe and reassured that I mattered; but I didn't live in a '90s TGIF sitcom. In the real world, **we are flawed people raised by flawed people,** and our best attitude to address that with is to be aware of those flaws and break our patterns of behavior.

Many of us grew up feeling like we had to DO things to earn the love of those who mattered the most. Most of the time the love we thought we were earning was actually just attention. That chase for attention doesn't go away when we get older, instead it compounds and grows exponentially, especially in an age of social media, where we can quantify the "love"[*] in likes and comments.

There's nothing wrong with us for getting caught in this cycle; it's natural. Humans are creatures of comfort, and comfort for us will be the things that feel

---

[*]   Aka attention

the most familiar, even if they're not the healthiest. As kids, when we had experiences that were uncertain and unfamiliar, we would run back to our parents or another safe place, something more certain and comfortable, and without some self-awareness, that pattern doesn't change.

As adults, when things feel too uncomfortable, uncertain, and overwhelming, we may not have a parent to run to anymore, but we have familiar spaces and habits. Those spaces and habits may not be the best for our growth, but they're what we know. For some it's the arms of an ex, or the bottom of a glass. For others it's comfort food, or friendships that hold a lot of history. This is understandable, even if we all have different triggers for discomfort, uncertainty, and feeling overwhelmed. The pattern remains, we'll stick to what we know, even if what we know isn't the best for us.

Life begins outside the comfort zone, but we're setting ourselves up for failure if we think we can just dive headfirst into a totally new situation without a plan in place for when things get out of hand. We'll only send ourselves back to the places we no longer want to be, because as bad as they are, we recognize them. That's what is referred to as **self-sabotage—picking familiar misery over unfamiliar happiness.** Our first step is to see this pattern, and to give ourselves space to be human and make these mistakes. The issue isn't always that we're weak and can't handle new situations; it just may be that we're taking too big of a dose and need to start smaller. Instead of the full head-dive into a new space, then fizzling out, let's work to have one foot grounded in the world we know and a foot exploring the unknown.

This means recognizing that we can't go hard at the gym on day one, we have to work our way up there. We can't toss all the junk food out of the kitchen, instead we should adjust one part of one meal until eventually we've made minor but manageable adjustments to our diet. Breaking old, toxic habits is important to receiving and realizing more love in ourselves, but it has to be done slowly, deliberately, and with a lot of compassion and patience.

We can't take the training wheels off immediately when we decide we're going to choose something new over what we've always known. Recognizing that we choose familiar over happy is an essential first step.

This partially explains our mommy and daddy issues. Our parents are often our first exposure to a relationship, and that models what we think they need to be, no matter how functional and happy their actual relationship was. Even as adults who can go back and analyze those relationships, on an emotional level, we recognize the familiarity and comfort when other people make us feel the way our parents did, and we're drawn to it. This is why cycles of abuse can continue, why codependence forms, and why we can often overcompensate with a partner for what we didn't get as children—because even our childhood fantasies can become comfort zones we chase and protect.

If Dad was hard to impress and you were always longing for more attention, don't be surprised if the guys you find attractive share that quality. Someone who pays you attention may seem foreign and weird. Recognizing this pattern early is important, before we pass on some of the best relationships we could ever have, just because we're choosing to stay in a loop of dysfunction because it's familiar.

This is why working on our relationship and exploring ourselves is essential, because that informs every other relationship we have. And seeing how much we subconsciously veer toward what we've always known is an essential first step to taking back the steering wheel and directing ourselves toward what we actually need. There's nothing wrong with us for being caught in these patterns, it's part of being human; but it's not a jail sentence. **The first step to breaking an old pattern that no longer serves us is admitting it exists.** After that, be kind and focus on the baby steps you need to take to go in a better direction. The willingness to do this work to break old patterns is a beautiful gesture of love that will widen its pathways within and around you.

WE ARE FLAWED PEOPLE RAISED BY FLAWED PEOPLE.

22.
LOVE IS FEELING IT ALL

We are life having a human experience, and that experience includes unpleasant feelings, from tummy aches all the way to existential dread. The issue isn't so much ridding ourselves of these feelings as it is accepting the fact that they're a normal part of existence. I've gotten in trouble in the past when talking about self-diagnosed depression, but I think it's important that we don't throw around the word *depression* lightly. Depression is real, but I strongly encourage you to seek assistance from a medical professional before labeling yourself.

For those of us who aren't dealing with deep-seated crippling depression, every color in the rainbow of emotions we have in our lives matters, is worth paying attention to, and serves a purpose. Feeling emotions doesn't mean we understand them, nor does it mean we can trust them all the time. To feel "off" is to assume we know what it means to be "on." Emotionally, our ideal state is neutral, not some everlasting euphoric condition where we're constantly in some blissful nirvana, although that makes for great marketing. We don't learn from happiness, and at our happiest moments, we can also end up making the dumbest mistakes. We've all been caught up in great moments with people and then we make great plans and promises and never follow through once we return to Earth.[*] So let's not think we're somehow failing in life if we're not happy all the time.

---

[*]   Aka sober up

On the other hand, it's not the greatest feeling to be in the dumps, and we shouldn't make any big decisions then either, but there's still a lot to learn during those emotional lows. **Love for self is holding space for these emotions to exist and run their course, because once they do, all that's left is the experience of love.** It's a nonobvious but very obvious fact that all of our emotions are temporary, both the pleasant and unpleasant ones. We can't stay mad for very long, nor can we remain jubilant. Our sadness can seem to stick, but its most intense moments don't exist in a marathon.

Loving ourselves isn't telling ourselves we shouldn't feel these ways, it's understanding that everyone is going to feel all the emotions at one point or another, and to hold space, pay attention, and let them pass.

Yes, it seems like the shitty feelings last longer than the wonderful ones. I vividly remember being a five-year-old child when my mom lost one of her brothers. The house was full of family members and people I didn't know crying. I had never met this uncle and barely understood death, but the moaning and wailing that seemed to go on for days had me feeling very unsettled. I remember daydreaming of hugging my mother and everyone cheering up, and we all lived happily ever after.[*] Since then, I've done my best to tiptoe around, duck, and avoid all unhappy feelings.

As I get older, I realize that there's value in feeling the lows and releasing emotion. A good scream, ugly cry, or shit breaking feels good every so often. I've also learned not to believe everything I feel and I can respect that my emotions relate not just to my circumstances, but also to my diet, the company I keep, the content I consume, and how much sleep I get.

I've also learned about shadow work, which is voluntarily going back and revisiting the darkest, most traumatic memories I have. By doing so I'm able to

---

[*] I probably saw something like that on TV.

give those experiences new context and process them with new tools I have, even tools as simple as intentional breathing.

Our emotions are all important, and we have to abandon the idea that only some should be welcome over others. When we hold space and surrender to the feelings that come our way, their impact lessens, for both the positive and negative, and we can find more peace in the neutral; that peace is love. This can be enhanced with journal writing, meditation, exercise, changes in diet, and getting a few more hours of sleep.

Love itself is a feeling we crave, and often we can get it wrong. There are so many bootleg feelings that we can mistake for love, like attention, status, power, and validation. Risking a counterfeit encounter is more reason to slow down and soak in all that's being felt before labeling something love.

This constant inner battle we seem to be fighting is exhausting, and the fortresses we build to "protect" ourselves will also trap us in and keep wonderful things out. So let's open the door, put out the welcome mat, and feel what needs to be felt. It's one of the best parts of being human, and an important part to keeping the flow of love moving in and around us.

TO FEEL "OFF"
IS TO ASSUME
WE KNOW
WHAT IT MEANS
TO BE "ON."

23.

LOVE IS ALWAYS TELLING THE TRUTH . . . TO YOURSELF

I have the word TRUTH tattooed on the side of my hand. I got the tattoo at a time in my life when I needed a foundation to stand on, as it felt like the rug had been pulled out from under me. Truth was something that no one could ever steal, and I committed to always telling the truth, no matter the consequences.

Then on a shopping date, a female friend asked me if the dress she had tried on made her look fat.

We look at lies differently depending on if we're lying or being lied to.

When we look at lies that have been told to us, they're horrible, hurtful, manipulating, and deceiving.

When we look at the lies we tell, we're just protecting ourselves and others from humiliation, shame, rejection, losing respect, and feeling unworthy.

I'm not here to attempt to solve the eternal question of "does this dress make me look fat"—some mysteries are better left untouched. I can't guarantee complete honesty and openness will widen a pathway of love between you and another person, because, honestly, I don't know any of you.

We can only speak as much truth as we can hear and accept.

Yes, being anything but truthful is draining; it denies us our authentic selves, and the peace that comes with it. Not being honest also keeps us from expressing and getting what we want. It keeps us in the prison of trying to be "perfect." Knowing that, the inconvenient truth still is, keeping it real can go wrong.

I've shared my real feelings in intense emotional moments, and it's bitten me in the ass.

I've shared my true feelings after rehearsing, proofreading, and rewriting before hitting send, and that also bit me in the ass.

So instead of telling you to always admit to someone you care about that you think someone else is attractive, or that they put too many onions on their burger, let's start at home.

The more honest we can be with ourselves, the fewer masks we have to wear, and the more of those truths we can share with the world.

That requires us to first admit we lie to ourselves, and then figure out why to break the pattern.

We lie to ourselves because we haven't developed the psychological strength to tell the truth and deal with the consequences yet. The more unpredictable and uncontrollable our lives feel, the quieter and less authentic we become. There's a lot of intimidation, anxiety, and fear around being seen, especially since we're not perfect, so we use lies to protect ourselves from potential pain, not realizing that lying to ourselves causes more pain and regret in the long run.

Here are some of the ways we often lie to ourselves:

- Denial
- Rationalization: justifying our bullshit
- Projection: projecting who we are onto others
- Thinking in extremes: it's either this or that, it can't be anything in between
- Thinking our feelings reflect our reality: since I feel like shit, life must be shit
- Making overgeneralizations
- Avoiding realities of life: death, the meaninglessness of life beyond what meaning we give it, the fact that we're alone, the relationships between our choices and responsibilities
- Maintaining cultural norms that go against our authentic selves

All of these have been put in place and practiced forever to keep us from having to face uncomfortable and uncontrollable realities of life. This most likely came from childhood, as coping mechanisms to handle ourselves in a world we didn't understand. **The ways we dealt with issues in childhood are the examples of the lies we tell ourselves as adults.** We take moments of pain and tattoo them into our psyche and then do the most to validate those truths. If someone made us feel ugly when we were young, we'll hold on to that belief like a comfort blanket and do everything we can to avoid feeling its pain, which may include telling ourselves that we're ugly before anyone else can.

To be honest with ourselves means we have to muster up the courage to speak, hear, and absorb truth, no matter how unpleasant it is. **We don't get stronger by only focusing on the pretty parts of life.** We get stronger by doing hard things, including being our authentic self. So instead of using lies to protect ourselves when shit hits the fan, let's focus on being truthful and self-aware.

> *"Choosing authenticity means cultivating the courage to be imperfect, to set boundaries, and to allow ourselves to be vulnerable; exercising the compassion that comes from knowing that we are all made of strength and struggle; and nurturing the connection and sense of belonging that can only happen when we believe that we are enough."*
> —Brené Brown

Honesty is taking full responsibility for who we are, because when we don't, we hurt ourselves and others. We need to practice observing ourselves and becoming more self-aware. That means when things feel overwhelming, when we contradict ourselves, when we think irrational thoughts, or when we feel hurt by others, we ask an important question: "What does this say about me?"

When we can be honest about the lies we tell ourselves, using compassion and understanding instead of judgment, we widen the pathways of love in our life. We stop trying to be perfect so often, and we can both speak and accept more truth toward and from others.

So does that dress make you look fat? If it does, that just means there's more of you to love.

;)

WE DON'T GET STRONGER BY ONLY FOCUSING ON THE PRETTY PARTS OF LIFE.

24.
SELF-CARE IS NOT ALWAYS SELF-LOVE

One awesome thing that happens when I'm in my book-writing season is that I stay in one spot and establish a routine with my writing, and that allows me to schedule other useful activities around that. This time, that's involved working with a personal trainer, yielding some great results. I lost my travel tummy, as I was no longer dependent on McDonald's for breakfast, and I'm getting more consistent sleep. Not living out of a suitcase has allowed me a solid skin-care routine, and the ability to drink more water, and cook all* my meals.

Some days I work out because it feels great, other times I do it because I want to look great, and the distinction is important. Although I've made progress and can probably justify a stomach tattoo in a few more months, I don't necessarily always feel better about myself, despite all this self-care.

That's because **although self-love involves self-care, not all self-care leads us toward self-love.** We can easily send ourselves down a rabbit hole of self-indulgent behavior designed less to make us feel good and more to stomp out the feelings we have of not being "enough." That *enough*

---

* Yes, all.

word is something you've seen throughout this book, and it's a key idea in understanding what it really means to love ourselves. Self-care can take us into the trap of trying to feel like enough, when self-love lets us know it's okay to be what we are, where we are. **With true self-love, there is no idea of enough.**

Self-love is deeper than self-care, it's a path in the direction of self-acceptance, and that acceptance is important because it frees us from judging the self-care we need. Self-care can often lead to us focusing on where we need improvement—maybe we have weight issues, or bags under our eyes, or our résumé is thin. Although it's important to make progress in life, there really is no pot of gold at the end of that rainbow. Self-love is focusing on accepting both our lovable and unlovable parts.

Where self-care fixes and addresses problems, self-love is the deeper reminder that we're not broken, and therefore there's nothing to fix.

Self-care can help our bodies, our spirits, our minds, our bank accounts, and the overall landscape of our lives, but self-love is what's going to help with how we feel. Both sides of the coin are interrelated, and feeding one will help with the other, but self-love won't run the risk of falling down a slippery slope. Self-love is self-correcting, whereas self-care still hints that there can always be more, and we can spend our whole life chasing.

Self-love feeds and informs self-care; self-care doesn't always do the same for self-love.

Self-care is having that overdue ugly cry; self-love will be cleaning up afterward.

So despite reading all the books in the wellness section of the bookstore, doing all the workouts, using all the creams, soaking in all the Epsom salts, and drinking all the wine, work toward realizing that you are wonderful as you are, and these are bonuses and maintenance but not requisite for you to feel like you deserve love; they happen BECAUSE you deserve love.

To have self-love also involves loving others, and receiving love from others. Those are past the point of self-care and are important to acknowledge. **Self-care won't make you love yourself, it should come from the fact that you already do.**

WITH TRUE SELF-LOVE, THERE IS NO IDEA OF ENOUGH.

25.

BE KIND TO YOUR INNER CRITIC

For South Asians, it's a very simple saying:

Lokh kee kahain ge?

What will people think?

Pound that into a child's head long enough, and they'll begin to think it was a thought of their own.

We all have thoughts, but that doesn't mean we actually did the thinking to create those thoughts.

Our inner voices often used to be an outer voice we absorbed and adopted as our own. Those voices trick us into believing outdated and straight-up dumb shit that we think is a part of our identity. Oftentimes, the people who planted the seed for those voices didn't realize they were doing it. We're all guilty of it. I once made an offhand comment about a loved one's outfit and never realized they threw the clothes away after that day. I didn't know the power of my words and the impact they had on someone that cared about what I thought.

I planted a seed that made it difficult for them to see the beauty in an outfit they were once excited about. As I move on with my life, that inner critic, if left unchecked, would grow inside of them.

The secret to checking these voices isn't to fight them with more negativity, it's to understand where they came from and respond to them with your truth.

Lokh kee kahian ge played a big part in me hesitating to leave my job as a teacher to be Humble The Poet, and at first my response was *"Fuck what everybody thinks, including you, Mom and Dad, I'm going to do me!"* But that only yields more conflict and stress.

Now when my inner critics speak, I recognize where they are coming from. I take the time and speak to myself aloud and say something with love like, "I understand it's scary to stray from the flock, and being an artist isn't the most reliable source of income, but I have to make choices for my life, and other people may not be okay with that, but that's fine, I'd rather fail by my own choice than be stuck living for others."

Again, these voices are manifestations of fears, ours and those of others; there's no point in adding any more aggression to the situation. Don't combat the voices, check them, let them know they're heard, but you're moving regardless. I'm going to sound like a broken record, but it's important to remind you that this is going to take daily practice. The more you do it, the better you'll get at it, and eventually it will be your default to dealing with your own inner critic.

Don't beat yourself up for beating yourself up.

Punishing ourselves for not being nice to ourselves only makes things worse. This takes time and A LOT of practice.[*] You're dealing with your inner ego-toddler here, and as with any toddler, patience is essential, alongside hugs, kisses, and love. **You don't have to solve these problems to be able to feel love from yourself; you have to feel love from yourself to be able to solve these problems.**

When we're kinder to ourselves, we can be kinder to others, and the love that flows within and in between us will have fewer hurdles to deal with. It starts within and will spread around you. I've been doing it for years with amazing results.

> *"Remember, you have been criticizing yourself for years and it hasn't worked. Try approving of yourself and see what happens."*
> — Louise L. Hay

---

[*] Did I mention the importance of practice before?

DON'T BEAT YOURSELF UP FOR BEATING YOURSELF UP.

26.

PROGRESS IS A GREAT FRIEND OF LOVE

Things don't have to be perfect for love, but often we think they do, and that belief suffocates love out of our lives. We think we're not good enough as we are and we have to be perfect. We think our heroes are perfect (even though they never are), and that leads us to believe that we have to be as close to perfect as possible to realize any love in our life.

It's time to divorce *perfect* and focus on *progress*.

Chasing perfection only leads to opportunities to criticize our imperfections, which hurts our self-esteem and feeds our insecurities. **The more insecure we are, the less love we'll realize.** Perfect is an abstract idea that really only exists in our imaginations or describes people we don't know well. Perfection is a useless goal, and as goals go, it also doesn't encourage much growth.

We have this idea that we aren't good enough; it's a complete lie that slowly fades with age, because we gain comfort in who we are and realize that the expectations we place on ourselves, or that we feel society places on us, were never realistic to begin with.

Someone can appear perfect on a social media post because the picture can be manipulated to hide all their imperfections—those imperfections that make them human. As we spend more time on these platforms, we catch ourselves comparing our real self to these fake highlighted lives and feeling like we need to also live that way before we can truly feel any love.

Instead, when we focus on progress, we are focusing on movement, which is growth. **Let's get better for the sake of getting better, and not because we think we're not good enough.** Let's aim in the direction of our potential and be okay with the idea that the journey toward our potential is never-ending. It's a journey without a destination, and we'll only stop making progress when we die.

If we were perfect, there would be nowhere to go and nothing to do. **Perfection is boring, while progress is adventure.** Instead of us setting these invisible finish lines or expecting things to go flawlessly on the first try, let's set directions and intentions, and decide that things steadily improving is better and more realistic than things ever being flawless.

When we decide to prioritize progress over perfection, we're deciding to make more space for love. We're okay that everything isn't ideal, and finding excitement in taking ourselves in the direction of "better." Getting better is not only good for self-esteem, it's amazing for self-respect, which makes us focus less on what others think about us.

Love requires connection, and that means seeing someone, relating to them, and caring about them. That would be next to impossible with anyone who's perfect. **It's our flaws that open opportunities to be vulnerable and connect with others on a deeper level.**

Focus on making progress every day, little baby steps in the right direction. Knowing how far you've come will motivate you to keep going and give you things worth celebrating and loving.

PERFECTION IS BORING, WHILE PROGRESS IS AN ADVENTURE.

27.

LOVING YOURSELF IS HONORING ALL OF YOURSELF

There are parts of us that are easy to love—it might be our helpful side, our sense of humor, or the fact that we share our Netflix password. There are also parts of us that aren't as easy to take. For me, that's my moodiness, my over-thinking, and whatever creative ways I use to make things difficult when my insecurities are holding the steering wheel.

If we had it our way, we'd only have these wonderful lovable elements, and all things others (and we ourselves) don't approve of would get phased out, like one-hit-wonder pop songs and viral Internet challenges. This is why we are in constant need of improving ourselves; it may even be the reason you bought, borrowed, or stole this book.

We hope the newer version of us will be better and therefore more worthy of love, but we'll never really feel that love if we can't love and honor who we are right now. We should all strive for progress and expand our mindsets beyond where they are, but we'll need to make space and time to mourn our mindsets of the past; otherwise, they'll continue to hang around.

Old relationships have taught us to be the new person we are today, and newer relationships will take this version of us and flip it upside down until we grow into a newer identity. Sometimes, we look back with a face-palm, wondering how we could have ever been so narrow-sighted and naive, filling ourselves with regret and resentment. No matter how much better we get, we may fall into the trap of lamenting how bad we were, and that's because we haven't made it a priority to see those old versions of ourselves as important steps on our journey to getting us to better places.

The old me is not my enemy, they're an important friend who helped develop the person I am today. The person I am today will not be obsolete as I continue to evolve.

Instead they will be an important shade in my gradient of growth.[*]

The version of me that thought my ex was my soulmate wasn't an idiot, he was a nice, endearing guy trying his best to figure things out. He had blind spots, but so does this current version of me, and I won't realize them until later in life. This is going to be an ongoing pattern for various versions of ourselves, each one deserving attention, honor, and respect.

Our yesterdays prepare us for our tomorrows, they're not just here to haunt us. When we can love all the previous versions of ourselves, we can love all the things about our present version, even the parts that feel unlovable. To love is to love all; when we make exceptions, we begin closing the pathways to love.

I don't miss all the past versions of myself, but I'm glad I went through them. I can't skip steps on my journey, and as painful, awkward, and outright embarrassing some sides of me have been, they mean just as much as my great qualities, like my ability to charm one of you into sharing your Netflix password.[**]

---

[*]   You can't skip steps in a gradient.
[**]   E-mail it to me.

THE OLD ME IS NOT MY ENEMY, THEY'RE AN IMPORTANT FRIEND WHO HELPED DEVELOP THE PERSON I AM TODAY.

28.

LOVE YOUR TRUTH >
YOUR RELATIONSHIPS

In my early 20s, I worked as a full-time elementary school teacher, and then I would do four hours a night of private tutoring to high school kids. By the time I was done, it'd be 10 P.M., and I'd head over to a friend's studio and work on all things creative until 2 A.M.. Then I'd get home and wake up at 7 A.M. to do it all again. It was taking a toll on me, and the only thing I should have been doing was creating art. But "coming out" to my parents with that idea felt terrifying. I didn't grow up in an authoritarian household by any stretch, but the thought of disappointing my family still crushed me. When I finally told them I was leaving my job to pursue art full time, they weren't happy, but they didn't stand in the way. I think they saw the time I was investing into it and the sleep I was sacrificing and realized I wasn't asking permission or seeking approval, I was honoring my truth.

I've molded myself to have people like me. I've done it to keep relationships alive, I've done it to get opportunities. I've even done it just to avoid conflict. Relationships are important, easily one of the most valuable parts of life, but when they come at the cost of our truth, it's not a fair trade.

Being anything other than who we authentically are is not a sustainable way to keep a relationship. A foundation based on anything but the truth is not a foundation, it's a temporary support that will crumble over time. We can only wear a mask for so long before it starts to suffocate us or we get lost in it. Maintaining our social contracts like this is going to eventually chip away at our being and leave us doing a whole bunch of unhealthy things to compensate.

Yes, keeping the peace is important, but resentment still festers. Just because we don't say things aloud to others doesn't mean they aren't said in our head, and the seed of damage from that resentment will start to sprout.

Let's not trap ourselves in relationships that don't align with our truth, and to do that we have to continue unearthing what our truth is.

This will not be the part of the book where I tell you YOUR truth, or what it should be. I can only tell you what your truth should feel like; it should feel right.

Your truth is your gut—trust it. Our instincts aren't always correct, but they're more correct than any other force we can experience. If something doesn't feel right, it doesn't feel right, and that's worth listening to. When we enter relationships that don't feel right, whether it's for a school project, friend-ship, or a life partner, we have to listen to those feelings inside us. So often, we suppress our truth because we're afraid of it. But that fear takes us away from love, and also ourselves. Your truth can be seen as your most authentic self. Much of the damage we cause ourselves in life is because we don't get to be our true selves.

Our true selves may not work well with the people around us; that's inconve-nient, but that doesn't make it any less of a truth. Trying to be anything other than who we are for others won't last very long, and the things that we do to suppress our own feelings of frustration and loss will only make things worse. **Pleasure is what we chase to replace the peace we can't achieve;** being ourselves will allow for more peace and less energy expended toward chasing pleasure.

It's a corny cliché to say, "Those who don't like you for who you are were never really your friends," but it's true.[*] There are moments when I've discovered my truth about something but have been too afraid to share it. I was afraid that when people saw the real me, I would be judged, shamed, guilted, and rejected. Being someone else seemed easier than being alone, but that's only true for a short time. Being someone else ends up being the reason we feel alone, even if other people are around.

We can lose ourselves trying to keep everyone else around. Settling for a life outside our truth leads to other destructive behavior and further damages our self-respect, which then has us chasing more outside validation to keep our ego-toddler from having a meltdown.

We can't share our truths if we don't know them, and we'll never fully know them, but that just means we should be on the journey to discover as much as possible. The first thing I recommend is to start with your needs, however superficial, silly, or strange. Figure out what YOU need, not what others tell you. Much of life's tug-of-war is between what we need and the script the world has written for us. There are plenty of instances where society, culture, the government, religious leaders, and our parents' generations have lied to us, or just been flat-out wrong about life. That's enough evidence to trust our own instincts about where we need to be in our lives.

If you like girls but everyone else likes boys, it can be hard to share that, but it'll be even harder to keep it hidden while maintaining a level of healthiness. The stress will manifest itself and chip away at you. Maybe you don't want to get

---

[*]   Clichés are played out for a reason.

married or live in the city you're in, or keep your hair color the way it is. Maybe you don't want to eat animals in a family that barbecues regularly, or you want to study modern dance instead of modern medicine. I don't know your truth, and frankly it's none of my business.[*] I'm here to remind you that you'll feel 10,000 pounds lighter and unlock 10,000 times more love when you live that truth.

It may be an expensive transition. I have friends whose parents still don't talk to them for coming out as part of the LGBTQ+ community. I have friends who left it all behind to be who they needed to be. The price of losing others who don't approve of your truth feels heavy in the beginning, but I can promise the weight of living a lie is much heavier in the long run.

As we discover ourselves, we need to communicate that to those in our life. It's scary, but it has to be done. You'll be surprised at how many people are okay with you being you, and how much that will inspire them to be them. I don't fit the mold of life, but that's because it wasn't my mold. **My relationships are important, so I know the difference between compromising with others to keep the relationship strong and compromising myself to keep it alive.**

When we focus on our truth and prioritize it over the expectations of others, we'll build more empathy for others to do the same and no longer require them to satiate our little ego-toddler. That might mean nontraditional romantic relationships or unique friendships without over-the-top expectations or loving family members deeply, but only from afar.

Living our truth builds our self-respect, which widens the pathways that connect us to love within. The more of our truth we discover and share, the more love we'll experience. The more love we experience, the more love we'll share, and the less outside validation we'll have to chase.

---

[*]   Or concern

When you find folks, partners, and situations that allow you to be authentic, you don't have to work so hard. There's little need to sacrifice yourself to keep things intact, and the love will flow in abundance. This isn't an infomercial promise for some ideal situation, you already have one or two of these relationships; I'm just encouraging you to double down on those more.

Don't be a martyr to keep others around, be yourself to keep yourself intact and full of love.

In Sikhi, the first Guru wrote *"Satnam,"* meaning "Truth is the only name worth uttering."

YOUR TRUTH IS YOUR GUT— TRUST IT.

29.

LOVE IS SITTING WITH PAIN

Want to experience love? Sit with pain.

I grew up in a house that had love and affection, but there was also a culture of "suck it up," and that created an imbalance between how much I took care of myself and how often I leaned on others for help. Truthfully, I only went to my family in emergency situations where I was in dire need, and they would always be there. But when it came to the little things—homework, a high school crush, not understanding my own emotions—I incorrectly assumed I had to deal with that stuff on my own. I wasn't used to leaning on others for much, and that in turn made me less welcoming for others to lean on; that meant I was less empathetic than the average bear.

The unfiltered straight talk that most come to love from Humble The Poet comes from that. I want to help, but I'm not very familiar with holding grace to hear the repeated complaints, and that started with me during my lowest moments. Now when others come to me with the same challenges again and again, I quickly try to remedy what ails them when often all they want is an ear to listen, maybe a shoulder to cry on, or just a hug. I always thought the weakness was on their end; now I know I hold some of it on mine.

But now I realize **to open pathways of love we need to build deep connections. Deep connections require empathy, and empathy requires us to feel and embrace pain.**

My lack of empathy was a direct result of me not wanting to feel pain, mine or others.

I struggle to sit with pain, and when it came to others, often it wasn't their pain that consumed me. Instead, their pain triggered my own. A friend recently moved and threw out all his stuff instead of taking it to the next place. He said most of the stuff just reminded him of a darker time and he didn't want to be triggered anymore, so he's starting fresh. That triggering is what happens to us when others bring their pain our way. Avoiding these triggers may help us feel better, but that also serves as a barrier in connecting with others, and ourselves, because the only reason we're emotionally triggered is because our own traumas have been left unaddressed for so long.

Sometimes the pathway to love is paved with pain.

That's nothing to feel bad about—it's a coping mechanism to bury our pain deep and do everything but face it. This way of coping is understandable, but it doesn't work very well. What we hide, or leave hidden in us, just pops out at our worst moments. All of this also creates blockages and congestion for the pathways of love in our life.

Because we don't like the discomfort of pain and trauma, we do so much to avoid, distract, and fix them. We think medicating, sedating, distracting from, and hiding our pain is the solution, but it's temporary, and in the long run it causes more damage. This also means we avoid others who may be going through pain, even though those vulnerable moments of pain are the essence of connecting through love.

We have to reveal in order to heal, clear out our emotional inbox, and whatever other catchy metaphors can be used to say that facing our pain is essential to experiencing love. We have to be patient with the flood of unpleasant feelings and discomfort until, at last, some beauty bubbles up from it.

It's so easy to distract ourselves these days, but that's counterproductive to who we are. We are human BEINGS, not human DOINGS, so being what we are is a better solution than doing something else to distract from it. We can't force pain away, that's not how it works, and by trying that, we end up creating more tension, which feeds that pain.

Remember, avoiding pain doesn't mean we're not feeling its consequences. We're all dealing with remnants of traumas we may not even remember.

If love is a priority, then pain has to be embraced, welcomed, sat with, and explored, no matter how much it sucks. "Suck it up" requires an endless capacity, and the more we hold in, the more will come out at the wrong time. Our only real salvation away from our pain is through it.

Here are some tips for sitting with pain in a mindful manner:

1. Acknowledge and Lean into the Emotion

Pain is often a message, so let's first acknowledge that something is being told to us, and from there we can figure out what that message is exactly.

The first step to dealing with an emotion is to be aware it's there. So often we feel strong emotions without being aware and acknowledging them. We skip straight to distraction to suppress the feelings. Instead, figure out what's being felt, and where it's felt. Is it pressure on the chest? A stomachache? A fast-beating heart?

Once we're aware of the emotion, we can turn toward it, face it, lean into it instead of avoiding it, pushing it away, or ignoring it. It can be helpful to look at the emotion as an alarm clock bringing something to your attention. The earlier we acknowledge the alarm ringing, the better the chance we have to improve from it.

2. Identify the Emotion OUT LOUD

Is it anger, depression, grief, anxiety, guilt, sadness, uncertainty, shame? Whatever the emotion, it has to be identified aloud. Instead of saying, "*I* feel anger" or, "*I* feel anxiety" separate yourself from the emotion and say, "*This* is anger," "*This* is anxiety." The emotion has to be acknowledged and identified, but that doesn't mean you own it. It's a moment we feel, not a moment we own.

3. Accept the Emotion

No one is excited to accept uncomfortable feelings, and to simply say, "accept the feeling" can be abstract, but it helps. I've taken magic mushrooms a few times in my life, and more than a few of those times have been unpleasant. Paranoid thoughts mixed with intense insecurities to make the experience very upsetting. I recently had a session with a shaman in a safe environment and was encouraged to accept all that was about to come my way. Before even taking a mushroom cap, I accepted I would have anxiety around stomach pains and embarrassment around throwing up. I also accepted that I might be terrified by the experiences I had under the medicine. This was new, because normally I fight everything and try anything to sedate the strong feelings.

With my acceptance came a more calming experience. **We create a lot of the tension in our lives fighting the unpleasant feelings that have yet to happen.** Accepting that they exist and not fighting them does a lot to reduce their intensity.

Accepting these emotions with kindness and giving them space to exist will do a lot to decide how long they'll stick around.

4. Remember, Emotions Always Pass

Emotions flow through us like a river or tidal waves, and we get to decide which ones we weather and which ones we surf. When we are feeling worse, remembering this fact is tough, so we have to remind ourselves when things are calm. This applies to both the emotions we want and the unpleasant ones. During these waves of emotions, we have options to fight them, embrace them, better understand them, or even ignore them.

Sometimes they pass after we have a heavy meal.[*] Other times they pass with a good night's sleep, a long run, a quick deep dive into silly Internet videos. The fact that you've experienced every emotion under the sun but you're not feeling them all at once at this very moment is enough proof that they'll pass.

5. Find Out the Trigger

Sometimes[**] I'm only crabby because I'm hungry, or sleepy, or both, much like a toddler. There was a perfect storm brewing, and then someone said something that triggered me emotionally, or I read something that pulled down my mood, or I stubbed my toe on the corner of the sofa. It's good to figure out the roots and triggers of our emotions so we can see the cause and effect and have a clearer view of the situation.

---

[*]   Sometimes they only occur because we're hangry.

[**]   Okay, more than sometimes

It starts with a simple question—*Why am I feeling this way?*—and through those conversations we can get into deeper questions like *Where did it first start? What can I do next time to be better prepared? How am I making things better or worse?*

This is an exercise in self-awareness instead of simply reacting to every-thing and anything that comes our way. We have knee-jerk reactions, but through identifying triggers, we can be better aware and equipped to deal with hard emotions.

6. Let Go

The sheer amount of frustration and resentment that come from trying to control something will often make things worse. The healthiest way to deal with uncomfortable emotions is to be open to them, feel-ing what we feel and allowing them to do what they do. This requires patience, which is a skill that takes practice. We'll have the urge to shut the feelings down, distract ourselves by looking at our phone, or medicate with a strong drink or another person's company. But if we do nothing and just sit with it, allowing it to exist, it will eventually burn itself out as long as we don't give it anything that continually feeds the fire.

7. Create Opportunities for Great Emotions

Sign up for a class, try a new restaurant; decide what happiness looks like and go for it. Take responsibility for the way you feel and create more opportuni-ties to have a healthier world outside and in. The more we exercise, the more stress we can deal with, the more new experiences we have, the bigger our minds grow, the more we'll be able to use our brains over our emotions when shit hits the fan.

This doesn't have to be a meticulous plan for happiness, it just has to be things that are energizing; from there, things will unfold as they may.

We can forever run from our feelings, but it's like being on a treadmill—we'll spend a lot of energy, but stay in the same spot. **If we don't deal with our feelings, they'll deal with us.** It's not a fight, it's an acknowledgment, a conversation, a coexistence. When we're able to stay in place* with pain, we'll punish ourselves less for feeling it, and we'll be in a better position to hear the pain of others without the fear of being triggered ourselves. These better positions will open up pathways of love that we feel even in the most uncomfortable times. **Love matters most when love is the hardest to find.** Sitting with pain makes room for that love to be discovered in and around us. It's short-term discomfort for long-term payoff, just like being at the gym or developing any new skill.

I have years of practicing sitting with pain ahead of me. I'm not perfect with it, I often make things worse before they get better, but I acknowledge that trying is better than not. **Pain isn't my enemy, it's an important part of my life, and easily one of my greatest teachers.** If I can continue to develop love for my encounters with pain, then I can continue to develop love for myself, all my flaws and triumphs included.

---

*   Be still.

SOMETIMES THE PATHWAY TO LOVE IS PAVED WITH PAIN.

30.

LOVING YOURSELF IS KNOWING WHO YOU ARE

I met Marquice, a retired professional football player, in Utah at an ice retreat which includes a bunch of outdoor activities in the cold, including ice baths and hiking up a snowy mountain in only our shorts.

The first night, as everyone was jumping into giant kiddie pools full of ice water, Quice said nope. Someone walked over to Quice and began to encourage him to join. Quice replied, "Oh I can join, I just don't want to." When I spoke to him the next day, he explained that he had done plenty of hard things in his life,[*] and he didn't feel the need to get in the ice water because he had nothing to prove. Marquice allowed himself to be himself and wasn't concerned about how that looked on the outside to other people, because he knew and loved himself.

It's normal to be afraid of loving yourself—the confidence that comes from it can easily be misinterpreted as offensive and cocky.[**]

---

[*] Only 0.00075 percent of high school football players will be drafted into the NFL.

[**] Probably why I originally named myself HUMBLE The Poet.

The opinions of others weigh heavily on us, and we are mindful of how we appear. To have love for ourselves can often lead us off the scripts and the expectations of others, and when we stand firm, that may rub some[*] people the wrong way.

Modesty and humbleness become the veil we cover ourselves with instead, not realizing it's a damaging disguise. We do it to avoid making others feel uncomfortable; it's an unspoken act we all put on that will surely trap us. There were other participants in Utah who didn't even consider saying nope as an option when our instructor told us to get in the ice water. Seeing Marquice do that didn't necessarily inspire them; some thought he was making excuses because he was scared.

The part that matters was, he didn't care.

Explaining is draining, and true confidence means you don't feel the need to explain yourself to other people. It's that lack of needing the validation of others that's the confidence, and it exists because that validation already exists within.

The popular misunderstanding of someone who really loves themselves is that they're a narcissist, but that's the furthest from the truth. **Narcissism is the opposite of self-love, it's a form of self-loathing.** Narcissism is relying on external validation, which is a sign of needing more self-love. Narcissists always have something to prove, and they display loud and selfish behavior. Confidence is quiet and calm; it's the act of being comfortable in your own skin, despite any flaws. **Real confidence doesn't come from being noticed, it comes from being better. Real confidence is modeling ongoing learning.**

As Tom Bilyeu says, "Don't try to be the smartest in the room, be the quickest to admit when you're wrong."

---

[*]   Most

Confidence is a by-product of self-love, and a rejection of the validation and opinions of others. **Confidence isn't proving you're worthy of love, it's knowing you are, and not worrying if anyone else does.** Confidence in anything requires practice, and that's life-long practice. Others who struggle with confidence may struggle to be around you, but that can't be a concern of yours. Modeling confidence can inspire them to pursue the same journey.

> *"Your playing small does not serve the world. There is nothing enlightened about shrinking so that other people won't feel insecure around you."*
> — Marianne Williamson

To love oneself isn't a loud, cocky proclamation, it's a peaceful realization, and much of it comes from acknowledging that it starts from the inside. Make noise only when it serves to help others; otherwise it's only going to further shrink you and make you depend on the opinions of others.

Marquise did eventually get into the ice, not because of peer pressure, but because someone else was hesitating and didn't want to go alone. He didn't have anything to prove to anyone, but he did have an opportunity to serve and support, and he took that opportunity. By then, most of the other participants had already gone inside to warm up, and that was fine with Marquice. An audience isn't necessary for him to grow and progress, he's been able to channel love from within to the point that it didn't matter if anyone else was around.

Some may not want you to be confident and better because it highlights their insecurities, but that's their problem, not yours. Don't dim your light because others can't handle the shine.

CONFIDENCE ISN'T PROVING YOU'RE WORTHY OF LOVE, IT'S KNOWING YOU ARE, AND NOT WORRYING IF ANYONE ELSE DOES.

31.

LOVE IS PUSHING YOURSELF . . . SOMETIMES

One of my lowest points was when I quit my job as a teacher to pursue art full-time and things weren't working out. I didn't have any money, the love of my life had broken up with me, and someone I had considered my best friend had betrayed me.

The music deal I quit my job for turned out to be fraudulent, and the friend who brought that deal my way disappeared. I lost my clarity, girlfriend, and best friend all within the span of a few months. I was financially ruined, heartbroken, and had no direction to my life. I spent weeks in bed taking whatever was in my medicine cabinet, avoiding the world, hoping for someone to come save me. And eventually someone did: me.

When I told that story for a long time, I thought the strong version of me emerged from a combination of J.Cole lyrics and an epiphany, but almost 10 years later, I realized it was something else: rest.

A favorite mantra for myself lately has been **"Learn to rest, not quit,"** and I think there's a lot packed into that idea. First, it helps get us out of this black-and-white mindset of our actions, recognizing there's a lot of gray in between. If something is not working out, that doesn't mean we have to quit, especially if we've made progress. Other options exist, like resting. This isn't the easiest mindset to adopt, considering all the pressure we feel from the world to be productive all the time, but we know it's the right mindset, because it feels like the right type of advice to give to someone we love.

My three-week chemical cocktail vacation during that low time wasn't the wisest choice for someone living alone. I could have seriously fucked myself up, but there was value to giving myself time to do nothing and process my next move. Not only does rest give us time to figure things out, it gives us the time to recoup to have the energy to act once we do.[*]

This is still something I struggle with because I'm always afraid I'm just romanticizing my procrastination and fear. I'm afraid I'm not resting, because it feels like avoiding, but that's where the trust comes in. **Self-love is knowing when you need to push forward, when you need to retreat, and when you just need to take a break.** It's not an exact science, and that's okay, our goal isn't to be right all the time, it's to learn and grow.

When I'm frustrated with something, feel like quitting, I remember my secret weapon: the word *yet*. This one word can do wonders to keep us going and working toward things we struggle with.

"I'm not a good writer . . . yet."

"I haven't hit my ideal weight . . . yet."

"I don't know how to ride a bike . . . yet."

"I haven't read a whole book . . . yet."

That *yet* is a big reminder that we're on a journey, and we don't come out of the box with all the skills and tools we need to navigate life, assembly is required.

---

[*]   Let's be clear, the three weeks of doing nothing was important, not the chemicals.

Most of the things we do have come from consistent work in school and with our families. We may not have noticed how gradual the progress was, but it was. When you were six, you wouldn't have been able to read this book. A systematic curriculum was made to teach you how to read slowly over 10 years. Imagine applying that to whatever you want to do.

Knowing when to rest is important, but love also includes a little bit of push. I think a good ratio is 80/20. Love yourself, be compassionate, kind, and aware of your needs and safety 80 percent of the time and kick your ass the other 20 percent. Think about lions in the wild—they spend most of their time sleeping and having sex with each other. Then once every few days, they go out on an intense hunt. Modern society has us thinking we need to be like robots, productive all the time and feeling guilty if we're not.

But we have more in common with the lions than the robots, so like lions, let's rest. That 20 percent can be as uncomfortable and unfamiliar as possible, knowing it's not your whole day, and it's just what you need to push yourself beyond where you are. **Progress is an important recipe for self-love, and in the world of progress, our only competition is ourselves.**

I've had days and weeks where I slept for only few hours a night and went hard working and hustling. And I've also had days and weeks where I binge-watched TV shows and taken three-hour walks. Both are good uses of time, and essential for my growth and self-love.

The rest is important, and so is the push. We want to always be improving, but it's got to be at a pace that is manageable, and any progress made, no matter how small, is worthy of recognition and celebration. **Don't be too hard on yourself for not doing a lot, but don't be too soft on yourself for not doing enough.** Self-love is both the push and the pull in the direction you need to head in at that moment.

SELF-LOVE IS
KNOWING WHEN
YOU NEED TO PUSH
FORWARD, WHEN YOU
NEED TO RETREAT, AND
WHEN YOU JUST NEED
TO TAKE A BREAK.

32.

LOVE IS COMMUNICATION WITH OUR DEEPEST SELF

When do we feel the most safe to be 100 percent honest in what we say? Around others, we have to censor ourselves to some degree, it's part of the social contract of civilization, and there's nothing wrong with that. But we have to create times to be able to talk about what's closest to our heart, to communicate with the deepest parts of ourselves without fear of judgment and rejection.

I think those opportunities exist best in our prayers. There's no need to lie and put up an image when praying. Regardless of your religious or spiritual beliefs, prayer is a very honest way to ask for help or a chance to say thanks. We can ask for and give thanks for whatever we want, and by doing so, we hold space for ourselves to keep it as real as possible. We grant space for ourselves to just be, which is the spirit of what love is. **Because our prayers are for us and no one else, they allow us to go deeper, be more vulnerable, and build a new level of intimacy with ourselves.**

Maybe the only way to connect with God is through the language of vulnerability, which itself is a dialect of love. Vulnerability builds stronger connections and levels of intimacy because there's no concern for appearing perfect and it frees us to explore our deeper selves. When no one else is in the room and we feel completely safe to be completely ourselves, we begin the journey of accepting who we are; that in turn helps us accept others just the same.

Journaling works well alongside prayer because there's a lot of value in getting words and expressions out of our heads. Often, thoughts are fragmented and the best way to make sense from them is to bring them to life, where we can see and review them. We have to protect our journals with our lives, because the moment we assume someone else may read them is the moment we'll no longer feel free to express what's really happening with us. **Radical self-expression is so important to strengthening the flow of love in our lives;** it should be held as one of the most important and regular things we do.

Where prayer asks for help and gives thanks, journaling can work in the places that exist in between. A friend of mine makes it a common practice to "write down the dark." He takes moments that have made him feel low, unworthy, and unhappy and he writes about them. They could be things that happened that day, or memories that were triggered from childhood. He voluntarily revisits the painful and unpleasant moments, and within them, is able to process the pain, and turn down the volume of emotions he felt about those dark times. These planned moments of communication with our deepest self strengthens our relationship with ourselves, which further opens the flow of self-love.

When we feel safe and strong enough to be that radically self-expressive, we learn so much more about who we are and allow ourselves to be what we are, and that translates into how we can interact and share love with others.

Keep praying, keep writing, keep expressing, keep loving.

RADICAL SELF-EXPRESSION IS SO IMPORTANT TO STRENGTHENING THE FLOW OF LOVE IN OUR LIVES

33.
LOVE IS SAYING NO

You'd think for someone's whose mother said no to him all the time growing up that I'd be much better at saying it myself, but I'm not. I struggle to say no to people who ask me for favors, I struggle to cut things short that aren't serving me, and I struggle to put my priorities and needs first over others, knowing that if they're not met, I'm not really of use to anyone else.

One of the hardest words to utter is *no*; it's a small word, but it's loaded. It's not easy to say no to other people, no matter who we are and what we've accomplished. Warren Buffett, one of the wealthiest humans to have ever lived, says he still struggles with saying no, but credits much of his success to it.

I understand why we fear saying no to others: it doesn't feel good to let people down. It also makes us look selfish and feel unlikeable, which makes us feel unworthy of love. I struggle with saying no to people, but I've gotten better at it. I realized that keeping everyone else happy only felt good in the short term and took a big chunk out of me in the long.

Let's make it clear, there is a bit of selfishness to saying no to others, but that just means we have to give new value to the idea of being selfish. Being selfish is important if you want to have any level of efficiency in life. If we can't express what we want or choose and honor a direction in our life, then we'll be stuck floating around, existing for everyone else but ourselves. Live like that for long enough and you start to feel lost, self-pity, and, worst of all, resentment. Resentment is a deep hole we don't want to fall into. It's very hard to experience any love when you're resentful of others.[*] That can be minimized by saying no.

It's not selfish to put yourself first, it's selfish to expect others to put you first. We're vague with what we want, especially around others, because of fear. We're afraid we won't get it, and we're afraid of being unloved by others because of it. If we don't choose a target, we can't miss, right?

If we're not clear with our needs, we'll be saying yes to everyone else's needs instead. Sure, that can make us feel like good people, martyrs, and have us living at the top of the selfless tower, but in the long run, it's just going to chip away at us.

Saying no is showing compassion to ourselves, which in turn helps us show compassion to others. Compassion is what we feel when we want to help someone who's dealing with something. The best way to practice this is to help ourselves when we're suffering. Saying yes to others is saying no to ourselves, and because of that, doing everything else for everyone else will keep taking its toll on us. Let's practice self-compassion, open the gates of love, and do what's needed for us to feel better.

Saying no also strengthens our self-respect and self-esteem. It allows us to trust ourselves and our decisions. Saying no means we're announcing we're worthy of having a happy life, and we know the boundaries that need to be honored to get there. Stronger self-esteem from saying no will lead us to take more risks, be more ambitious, and cope with loss or rejection much better— all the ingredients of a wonderful life.

---

[*]   Or yourself

Saying no teaches others how to treat us, it lets them know our boundaries and what they can cross and can't. Most of the time in my life, I've been afraid to say no to others, fearing their wrath, but rarely[*] did that happen. Instead, people started to better understand me and how to deal with me. People stopped asking me to do things they knew I wouldn't do, and that allowed me time, energy, attention, and love to put toward the things I wanted to do.

Being there for others is great, but there has to be a YOU for that to happen. Ensuring our needs are met is how we can ensure we can be there when it really matters to ensure the needs of others.

Saying no means we care about ourselves, our time, and what matters to us. That focus is important to realizing love that's always existed within us. To love means to support, and we need that support before we can support anyone else. Saying no is an important step in building that foundation of self-care, self-respect, self-esteem, self-worth, and self-love.

---

[*]   Not never

IT'S NOT SELFISH TO PUT YOURSELF FIRST, IT'S SELFISH TO EXPECT OTHERS TO PUT YOU FIRST.

34.
LOVE IS SHOWING YOUR TEETH

As a student teacher, I remember sitting in the vice principal's office. I had been working in the school for six months at this point, and my only goal was to get noticed so I could land a job, or at least a letter of reference. The vice principal had agreed to see me, and the point of the conversation was to gain insight about what I should do after I graduated, but also to get on his good side in case any jobs opened up at the school.

As I sat quietly, he explained to me the challenges of being a teacher, the fact that it's the only white-collar job where people can come to your work and yell at you, referring to the parents. He talked about the uphill battle of trying to educate in a world where politicians decided funding and policy.

I nodded and smiled. I wasn't too versed in politics back then, and my only real goal was to stay on his good side, and maybe say something that would make me stand out among the other student teachers at the school.

Then he said, "And now they're trying to make us teach the kids that it's okay to be homosexual, and that marriage can happen between two men. Well, not at my school!"

I was caught off-guard by his prehistoric comment, but I continued to nod and smile, while inside I felt like a part of my soul was coming loose.

When I got home, I felt like shit, a fraud, and I resented both that vice principal and myself.

That wasn't the only time I let something like that happen. If anything, that moment highlighted how often I chose being liked over being myself.

I've shrugged off racist comments, laughed at sexist jokes, and allowed myself to be the butt of jokes, all so I could be accepted, and I know I'm not the only one.

We're all guilty of compromising parts of ourselves so others will like and accept us. There's a part of us that wants to stand up for us, but we're afraid it's impolite and unlikeable, and we're right, it is, but that doesn't make it any less important.

Sometimes we think being harmless and not rocking the boat is what makes us a good person, but really that leads to more of these unpleasant situations, and when we don't handle them the way we should, resentment grows. That resentment feeds an ugliness within us and further closes any flows of love we have in our life.

We can always go home and rehearse what we should have said—a tactful way to ensure we're not used as a doormat or choose to be liked over being ourselves. But at the moment we're caught off-guard and since we only think about it after the fact, we'll continually be caught off-guard.

Bullying is when others impose their power upon you, and that's exactly what these situations are. We allow ourselves to be pushovers in the name of being accepted, not realizing that we're only accepted as a pushover. Standing up for ourselves and others means we have to risk not being liked.

The inconvenient truth is that others will continue to try to encroach on us until we set boundaries and show our fangs. If we continue to let others trespass on our values and our space, we can find ourselves being victimized repeatedly.

But I'm Humble, I don't want to bite anybody, I'm a good person.

Well, my handsome friend, if someone encroached on somebody you loved, you'd bite back in their defense. This is just a matter of remembering to love yourself as well.

Being lovable doesn't mean being likable.

Standing up for yourself doesn't mean you lack morals or want to be unlikable. Standing up for yourself means you love and care for yourself more than the approval of the people crossing the line in your life.

It's the kid at school who doesn't want to fight that ends up with the black eye. It doesn't even have to involve violence. People at school or work may be taking credit for your work, people at a party may only want you around so they can tease you. As civilized as we want to pretend to be, we have to embrace the fact that it's our job to let the world know we have fangs, and if they cross the line, they're going to get bitten.

Sometimes keeping it real will feel like it went wrong, but that resentment we feel toward ourselves when we don't honor who we are is causing more damage than any consequence we get from doing so.

I may not have spoken up to the vice principal out of fear, out of the fact that I'm not part of the LGBTQ+ community and wasn't personally offended, maybe it was shock, or maybe I was just young and would have agreed to anything to gain favor. But that was setting me down a path that would require me to continually compromise myself for the acceptance of others, which may have won me some acceptance, but would have made it impossible to look at myself in the mirror.

Once I began standing up for myself, I only lost favor from those people who didn't want me to have boundaries and needed to have power over me so they could feel good about themselves; losing those people doesn't feel like a loss at all.

Loving ourselves is showing our teeth, letting others know we have lines that can't be crossed. It may feel like we'll be seen as unlikable, but really it'll gain us respect from within and from others.

Recognize that showing your teeth is far less toxic than holding resentment and far healthier when it comes to keeping the flow of love in your life.

BEING LOVABLE DOESN'T MEAN BEING LIKABLE.

35.

BE WHAT YOU LOVE, NOT WHAT LOVES YOU

When I first started sharing my work with the world it was because I loved learning new things and sharing what I learned with anyone that would listen. I would read an article about a new study or come across a lecture on something philosophical or spiritual. I'd have my mind blown, and then rush to spread my new treasures. I'd share in one art form or another: music, prose, or even images I created or found online. Creating the art was gifting me more eureka moments and working out the new ways of thinking helped to create new and stronger connections with my audience. If I learned a new lesson about love, I'd write a love song. If I learned something new about a geopolitical situation, I'd pepper that into a post around social justice.

Sharing this work helped form a community, and I thought I was on track to have the ultimate life: making a living doing what you love. That is until I fell in love with something more intense than the creating: the attention.

Humble The Poet the creative made dope shit, but Humble The Poet with the big social media following got paid to wear clothes, use technology, and attend movie screenings. Creating was nutrition for my soul but being famous paid the bills and was junk food for my ego. The more people that knew of me, the more unique opportunities came my way. No longer was I an isolated creative taking deep dives into his interests and scribbling them down on my little corner of the Internet. Now I was playing the game of the attention economy, the more eyeballs the better, and it was no longer about sharing things that excited me, it was about figuring out what the people wanted.

I was no longer doing what I loved, I was doing what made people love me.

It was working, and I was earning, and getting stopped in the streets almost everywhere I went. I was more famous for having famous friends than for sharing warmth from the creative flame that kept me going in the early years. What I didn't realize is that fame isn't something that's sustainable, in the real world or from a mental health perspective. I began thinking I needed to do more to keep up my clout, otherwise it would fade. But that's like trying to grab onto a handful of water; the tighter I squeezed, the less I could hold.

The chase solution wasn't to get more famous, it was to get off stage and not chase fame at all.

The challenge with fame, status, and owning exclusive things is that they only matter in relation to others. I'm only famous in contrast to others, I only have status in comparison to others, my watch is a collector's item because no one else can get it. These gestures put our self-worth in the hands of others and they have us running on an endless treadmill to keep up.

These are zero-sum games,[*] and putting our worth behind them means that getting what we crave comes at the expense of another. There's only one spot on the top of *The New York Times* bestseller list, there's only one most-followed person on Instagram, there's only one winner for best picture at the Oscars.

---

[*]   If one wins, another loses.

Now Rupi Kaur begins to feel like less of an ally and more of a competitor. Getting mistaken for Jagmeet Singh becomes less flattering and more of a shot to the ego. Being told I was discovered through Lilly Singh becomes less a sense of pride and more resentment that I'm trapped in her shadow.

All the meanwhile I'm focused on these games, and not focused on what I love, learning and creating.

When we play these games, we become less about what we love and more about what loves us. **Being loved for anything but who we truly are puts us in a prison of being somebody else, and the longer we are trapped, the more of ourselves we'll lose.**

Instead, let's chase the things that make us excited, that make us not need validation because they give us those moments of inner peace and freedom we long for. I'm not going to get idealistic, I have to earn money, and if I write a great book, the world has to find out about it, and that requires getting attention, doing interviews, taking pictures, and being a public figure. But that doesn't have to be the be-all and end-all, and it doesn't require me to compete with others or lose myself in the process.

We are social creatures, and the approval of others matters. I'm not going to lie, but let's pay attention when chasing approval and status comes at the expense of us exploring and enjoying what we actually love. **Gaining attention and status is addictive, but not nutritious.** When we focus on what we love, we'll need them much less.

I'm writing this book about love because I want to widen the flow of love within myself, and as I learn how to do that, I'm here to share those nuggets with anyone who wants them. This is also a non-zero-sum game. The more I learn, the more I share, the more value others may find. The more value they find, the more they'll help me continue doing it. No one has to lose for me to gain. I don't have to play the game of trying to get higher on the fame hierarchy if I focus on fostering a community of people on the same voyage as me.

Let's spend time focusing on what makes us feel alive, excited, and full of love, and spend much more time doing that. We may not have to quit our jobs to do it or play any other games to keep it up. It may be coming home after work and building action figures, or working on a short film, or dancing the night away. Whatever it is, you have to discover it to do it, and once you do, almost everything else becomes easier, or irrelevant.

BEING LOVED FOR ANYTHING BUT WHO WE TRULY ARE PUTS US IN A PRISON OF BEING SOMEBODY ELSE.

36.
LOVE IS KEEPING YOUR COMMITMENTS TO YOURSELF

On a late-night walk through a haunted-looking forest in Poland, I huddled near Steve Weatherford because he had a flashlight and, well, he's a giant.[*] We had just met the night before on this Wim Hof adventure,[**] but it was clear that Steve was not only six-foot-three and 220 pounds of muscle, he was also a ball of light and love.

Steve has six kids, so when the topic of what important lessons he wants to leave with his kids arose, he said something that hit me hard: "I want my kids to act on their commitments, not on their feelings."

We all know the hard things we can do to make life better: wake up earlier, eat more vegetables, have less sugar, look at fewer screens; the list can be endless. But when it comes time to follow through, we can often fall short. That's because **the version of us who made the commitment to wake up early isn't the version of us who has to get out of that warm bed.**

---

[*]   His nicknames include "the White Gorilla" and "Building." See for yourself @weatherford5!
[**]   For those that don't know Wim Hof, he's a beautiful yet nutty soul who discovered the benefits of sitting in ice water to regulate our anatomic systems.

The version of us who gets a shot of dopamine just saying, "We should get together!" to a friend then disappears when it comes time to follow through, offering no motivation to actually schedule something.

When we make and then break promises to ourselves, we chip away at our trust and self-respect. We're all guilty of it, and although it's nothing to be ashamed of, we still may feel some shame. Just remember, that shame won't always motivate us to do better next time. Instead let's recognize it and try again.

Sometimes we feel like we've failed ourselves when dealing with others. Maybe we said we wouldn't take them back or wouldn't allow them to speak to us like that again, but often, we fall back on our old patterns. Breaking these commitments to ourselves breaks opportunities for us to feel love for ourselves, so let's try to make progress in the other direction.

When we act on our commitments, no matter how big or small, we feel better about ourselves. There's value to our word, to others and ourselves. **The more we keep our word and act on our commitments, the more momentum we create, and the better habits we can build.**

As Tony Montana so eloquently said in *Scarface*, "All I have in this world is my balls and my word, and I don't break them for no one."

Our word, our commitment, and our credibility matter both to the outside world and to ourselves. We can get away with justifying all the reasons our words and actions don't align for only so long before it takes a toll on how we feel about ourselves.

If we say we're going to do something, we have three options:

1. We do it.
2. We don't do it.
3. We can't do it and communicate that.

I'm guilty of breaking commitments of all sizes, from skipping out on social events, to remaining faithful in a relationship. Even when I got away with it, I didn't get away with it. I have to live with myself, look at myself in the mirror, and wonder if I can trust my own words. **Making a commitment to do better than before involved me having to own up to my past bullshit and make adjustments and have hard conversations, both with people I care about and myself.**

We can start small with our commitments, and honoring them will make us feel good about ourselves, and that momentum will allow us to slowly build our way up. If we're waking up at noon, let's not make a commitment to getting up at 6 A.M., let's start with a smaller change, 11:30 A.M., and slowly get to 6 A.M. If we said we're going to eat healthier, instead of throwing out the fridge, let's start one meal at a time, or even one part of each meal. Instead of committing to writing a book, commit to writing for 10 minutes uninterrupted and work your way up. No matter the size of the commitment, when we keep our word, we build trust among ourselves and with those who matter, opening up a pathway for love to flow more freely.

At the very least, let's always ensure we keep the promises we make to ourselves.

Steve and I walked and talked for so long, we got lost in the haunted forest, but we eventually found our way back. After the trip Steve said to me, "Humble, we have a lot of life left to live together, brother," and my heart filled with love, not only because I'm excited to spend more time with a new bro, but because I really believe him.

THE MORE WE KEEP
OUR WORD AND ACT
ON OUR COMMITMENTS,
THE MORE MOMENTUM
WE CREATE, AND THE
BETTER HABITS WE
CAN BUILD.

37.
THEY CAN ONLY LOVE US FOR YESTERDAY

When looking back, my life is a smorgasbord of triumphs and failures, and depending on what people can see, I'm either a wonderful human being or a piece of trash. I receive daily messages online from those who have connected with my work in some way. Some say it helped them get off an addiction, others liberated themselves from toxic relationships. None of this was my intention when I wrote those books. If folks met me at my lowest, the last thing they would do is make time to read anything I wrote.

It doesn't really matter if others admire us or loathe us, they can only form their opinion of us based on what we've done in the past, not who we are in the present. Everyone in our life and on the planet has a limited view of who we are and has to form an opinion based on that tiny glimpse. Their opinions will be based on limited information, mixed with their own biases.

We have the clearest view of who we really are.

The only way someone could see us as clearly as we see ourselves is if they became us. We can't really have informed opinions on why other people do the things they do unless we are completely in their shoes, skin, and beard. That's the moment we become them, and then we would be making those exact same choices they did, being them.[*]

Since everyone only has access to a few pieces of our puzzle, it doesn't make sense to value how one person sees the whole picture. They can only judge us for things we've done, and not who we've become as a result. The whole puzzle is always more important than the individual pieces, so let's reserve our opinions and not weigh the opinions of others too heavily.

By the time you're reading this book, this chapter, this sentence, this word, it's a part of my past, and although it reflects on who I was, it may no longer be who I am.

What we've done in the past is not the only thing that decides who we are, but it is the only thing others can see to have opinions about us, so let's stop worrying so much about what others think and chasing their approval. The chase for outside validation will leave us lost, confused, exhausted, and spinning in circles.

It's great to celebrate a person's accomplishments. I have favorite basketball players, artists, and thought leaders, but I understand that I'm only seeing a fraction of them and don't judge them too intensely based on what I see from my seat in the nosebleed section of their life.

This realization has taken a lot of pressure off me to impress other people and allowed me to move forward a little less impacted by their praise or criticism. The less I worry about the opinions of others, the freer I am to be my genuine self and focus on how I feel in my own skin, remembering that others don't get to set the bar for me, just as I don't get to set the bar for them.

---

[*]   You still with me?

I don't expect this chapter to instantly free you from the bonds of needing acceptance, but I do hope it gets you thinking about this from a different perspective. **We judge others on their behavior and ourselves on our intentions.** The reason we judge ourselves on intentions is because we know our intentions, we have that additional context. When we see what others are doing, that context is missing, and we have to start assuming we know why they make the choices they make. This is where choosing curiosity over judgment is important. If others choose to judge us more than be curious about us, that's their problem, and their ill-informed opinions are stuck with them, not us.

We rarely know others' intentions, and they rarely know ours. What I'm encouraging is that we spend this energy focusing on what's more within our view and control instead of trying to make others happy, as they may have already made up their mind about us a long time ago.

They can only love us for yesterday, but we exist in the now and make choices for tomorrow. So let's focus on the gift of our present, be the truest version of ourselves, and let that self-love flow in abundance.

SINCE EVERYONE ONLY HAS ACCESS TO A FEW PIECES OF OUR PUZZLE, IT DOESN'T MAKE SENSE TO VALUE HOW ONE PERSON SEES THE WHOLE PICTURE.

38.
LOVE WHO YOU ARE AND THE EXPERIENCES THAT SHAPED YOU

Years of debt, doubt, and thoughts of completely giving up on existence; that's how bad it got for me at the beginning of this journey as Humble The Poet. Things got better slower than a lazy snail, and with such gradual progress, I didn't really notice it, especially compared to how sudden and intense my failures and setbacks felt.

I don't want to look back at the last 10 years as some sort of tragic story I can sell to others, or as the cause for the traumas I carry. I want to see those experiences as the gifts and opportunities they were. Those things weren't done *to* me, they were done *for* me.

I'd be lying now if I said I was in a completely better place. With the different levels come very different devils. So now I'm constantly releasing myself of a promised "happily ever after" and instead adding the reminder of, "You've been through a lot, and you can handle going through more."

Everything we've gone through up until this moment is what created us as the magical people we are today. Those highs and lows make a perfect harmony to the soundtrack of our life, and they deserve a shout-out during our award speech.

We are not victims of our past traumas, we are students of them. Traumas don't need to be healed and forgotten, they need to be learned from and incorporated. They serve an important role in our development and should not be dismissed as mistakes or regrets. The fact that our mistakes repeat in our head over and over is a feature of the human experience to ensure we actually learn from it; that's a gift, not a curse.

> *"To live is to suffer, to survive is to find meaning in that suffering."*
> — Gordon Allport (or DMX)

WE ARE NOT VICTIMS OF OUR PAST TRAUMAS, WE ARE STUDENTS OF THEM.

39.

WHAT'S IN YOUR WALLET??

Our second date was to the staff Christmas party at the school where I was teaching. She introduced herself to the other teachers as my fiancée, and that caught them off-guard. I dared her to do it, and she played along. She had a danger to her, and it was exciting. Every so often, a colleague would walk by and whisper to me, "Your fiancée is gorgeous, where have you been hiding her?" and that would fill my wallet of self-worth with pride and validation.

We had created a theme of pushing past convention so early in our relationship. Within a month, we had already planned a three-week trip to Thailand, and every time I brought her anywhere, she would turn heads and we'd steal the show. My wallet was getting fatter.

She made me feel seen and heard. She was the first person to ever say, "The world needs to hear Humble The Poet." She pushed me to be a creative and live a life beyond what was familiar to me. On top of that, other people couldn't hide their admiration for her beauty, and although it was foreign, it was delicious and addictive to get so many compliments all the time. It made me feel rich.

It was one of the most important transformations I had in my life. We lasted about 18 months before her need for adventure took her overseas and she ended our relationship. The months leading up to her to moving away, I was an insecure mess, unable to figure out why I was so anxious, unable to communicate when I wasn't happy, only able to express intense emotions like a child. My tiny ego-toddler was having multiple temper tantrums.

She was filling my ego quicker than my heart.

She had become my source of self-worth and self-esteem, and if she was going to leave, so would anything I had of value—or so it felt. I considered her the only thing in my wallet of value, and because of that, I wasn't able to be myself. I was just a person who was always afraid of losing the one person that made me feel like I mattered.

Once she was gone my worst fears were realized: I felt like nothing without her. Everyone knew me as "the guy with the beautiful, social, exciting girl," and now, I was just "the guy." I felt like my best days were behind me, and I could never do better.

When we suffer loss in our lives, it's not just loss in a physical sense, it's also a loss to our identity. We may stop believing we're deserving or even capable of love, because the reasons we had love in the first place were external things. Maybe it was a beautiful partner, or a dream job, or a juicy bank account, or a reputation, or a large following, or status in the community, or even a sexy beard. We may have our identity planted in a religious or political belief, or a favorite sports team—it doesn't matter, what's important to notice is that they're all external things. Our identity and self-worth are planted in these things, and we get our value from them; but once they're gone, so are we.

After losing this person, I had to ask myself that question. What parts of me had any value if I didn't have her? We've all experienced these types of losses or can at least identify things that make us feel valued and, if lost, would do a number on how we feel about ourselves.

I didn't want to feel this type of loss again. I never wanted the rug to be pulled out from under me again. I wanted my self-worth and value to be based on things no one could ever take away from me. So I reorganized my wallet.

My wallet is now full of things that no one has the power to take from me, but instead only I can forfeit. The contents in my wallet are:

- My ability to love
- My ability to tell the truth
- My compassion
- My empathy
- My service to others
- My humor
- My ability to ask for help
- My creativity
- My optimism
- My gratitude
- My desire to build community

The contents of my wallet are the reason I have value, both to myself and others, and no one can snatch them from me. They are qualities that may not be evident to the outside world, but they have a presence that fills me up. It's not always easy, but I can use the stuff in my wallet whenever I want, and the best part of it all is that the more I use the valuable things in my wallet, the more of them I have.

Filling our wallets doesn't require anything but ourselves.[*] The key to self-love is acceptance, and as flawed as we all are, we all still have the ability to accept that we can be so much more than we currently are. Instead of searching for more valuable things around us, let's find them within.

This doesn't mean I don't have days where I feel like shit, this means I have a wallet full of choices I can exercise when I feel like shit to help turn things around. Practicing these things isn't always easy either, but doing difficult things feeds self-respect, which itself opens pathways of love in our life.

My wallet also lets me decide what's important to me when connecting with others. Does their presence feed the contents of my wallet or drain it?

Again, notice, I didn't put my net worth, notoriety, or semi-symmetrical face in my wallet as things of value. **I, like all humans, enjoy things that tickle my ego, but I understand how unsteady that ground is to stand on, and how it can all go away tomorrow.**

Money can dry up, partners and friends can leave, and beards can fall out. But no one can take away our ability to be honest, show love, serve others, or express gratitude. All of these, including everything else in my wallet, are priceless and remind me of how much value my life has.

So what's in your wallet? Where are you finding your value right now? What needs to go? And what needs to be included that can stay with you forever?

---

[*] Well, the metaphorical wallets anyway. I don't even own a wallet in real life!

WHEN WE SUFFER LOSS
IN OUR LIVES, IT'S
NOT JUST A LOSS IN
A PHYSICAL SENSE,
IT'S ALSO A LOSS TO
OUR IDENTITY.

365 PROPOSALS:
A *love* STORY

Kyle and Stu lived a block and a half away from us, and I'd crash at their place every now and then. They'd been living together for three years and had a beautiful home, and a synergy any couple would die for. These two are #couplesgoals in every sense, two great people, very different personalities, but somehow they complement each other in so many ways.

Stu sent an e-mail out to the friends circle, asking us to help him propose to Kyle. The plan was, on their morning walk, Kyle and Stu would run into us on their regular route and we'd join them. Eventually Kyle would pick up on the fact that all of his friends just happened to be at the same place at the same time, and then Stu would get down on one knee and propose.

It was an adorable proposal that never got to happen.

Instead, that morning, before they even left for the walk, Kyle picked up on Stu's strange behavior and confronted him, to which Stu replied by panicking and proposing right then and there in bed. Kyle said yes, and we all had a laugh when they told us.

The wedding was in Ojai, a hippie town north of Los Angeles, at a nondenominational temple that was more spiritual than religious. They took turns walking down the aisle, and what struck me was the urgency Stu showed to get to Kyle as soon as possible, as if they were reuniting after a decade. Even after living with each other for three years, he was as excited as ever to be near his partner. The vows were magical and had everyone in tears, and me wondering if I should hire these guys to ghostwrite for me. The reception was a blast, and I would consider it one of the best weddings I ever attended.[*]

Both too busy with their flourishing careers, Kyle and Stu delayed going on honeymoon, and life went back to routine after the wedding. They still lived a block and a half away, and they still went on their morning walks. But now, every morning, while on their walk, Stu would get down on his knee, and propose to his now-husband, and Kyle would say yes.

Every day, without fail, Stu would propose, and Kyle would accept.

These two don't live to create moments, they live in their moments. Their wedding was beautiful because the tears were real, the smiles were big, and the people attending wanted to be there. Stu didn't get his storybook well-orchestrated, surprise proposal. Instead, he got a partner who picked up on the signs that something was different, and they left the rest of us hanging while they got engaged in the comfort of the bed they shared.

Then they relived that love every day on their walks, a predictable gesture that did less to sweep Kyle off his feet and more to strengthen the foundation they stood on. **Pathways to love are paved with the things we do every day.** The investments of time, energy, attention, and focus add up, and there's something to show for it as time builds on.

---

[*]   I also hate weddings, so please don't take this as a sign that you should invite me to yours.

40.
THE CRAZY SHIT WE BELIEVE ABOUT LOVE

Sometimes it feels like we wouldn't know love if it wore a name tag and fell on top of us. The ideas, beliefs, and expectations we have around love have been influenced by so many places around us for so long that it's hard to know what's fake and what's real, and what role we need to play in order to recognize love.

The Disney movies we grew up watching sold us an idea that a guy must earn the girl through big gestures or by proving his worth. On the flip side it also plants the idea that the girl must be worthy of the guy trying to win her over. In addition to pushing outdated heteronormative ideas, this also teaches young people that they have to *earn* love. On top of that, the media tells us that getting love has to look and feel a certain way: love at first sight as cupid shoots an arrow into your butt, music swelling, and a wedding with birds and a baby deer carrying the train of the bride's massive wedding dress. This has a bunch of young people believing they are not worthy of love unless they do or become more than what they already are.

Being the knight in shining armor has evolved into needing a six-pack, a nice car, and some level of status over other guys. Being the princess in the tower now means being worthy of being wooed, waiting to be approached, and focusing on being desirable through looks and other superficial measurements.

Although Disney's gotten much better at telling stories with healthier lessons and celebrating different types of relationships, what we grew up watching had a big impact on us. The girls were the selectors, and the guys did the chasing. The big idea passed down is that we have to become something more than we are to be worthy of love.

Beyond the children's films, romantic comedies sell us stories of love at first sight and living happily ever after. These hyperinflated "realities," crammed into a 90-minute film, leave out the downtime and dead spaces that real life has. The media also reinforces the age-old idea of finding a "better half," assuming that finding love from another will somehow complete us, as if we're not a complete person to begin with. Remember that experiencing love from another person can't complete or heal us. Let's be more mindful of this and how it impacts the expectations we have around love and romance.

And then there's porn. **Porn does a lot to serve as the fast food of love.** It's easy, fast, and cheap, and too much of it will definitely have an unpleasant impact on how we feel about love, intimacy, and the reality of our relationships.

Someone longing, willing, and always wanting our attention is a few clicks away. They're always in the mood to put us first, and if they don't do it for us anymore, we can click on to the next and start all over. A study from the University of Oklahoma tracked couples over a six-year period to see what factors influenced the quality of their relationship and their satisfaction with their sex lives. The researchers found that of all the factors considered, porn use was the second strongest indicator that a marriage would suffer.[*]

---

[*] The most predictive factor was the "lagged dependent variable," which, even after Googling, I couldn't explain.

Love can't heal childhood wounds or make us enlightened. The experience of love can definitely fuel the journeys toward that, but that work is still up to us.

Our grandparents didn't do love better than us, their stories are just celebrated and romanticized with a nostalgic eye. This sepia-toned romantic view of love in the past is also something we have to let go of. Generations before us grew up in different times, but people are people, and they've always had problems. Context matters, even when talking about "the good old days." Our grandparents' generation wasn't isolated the way we are, and both the opportunities and external stresses[*] pale in comparison to what we're feeling today.

Just because they stayed together for 50 years doesn't mean they can be seen as the benchmark for love. There's a lot to learn from them, but Grandma wasn't competing with other girls on social media, and Grandpa wasn't battling FOMO as he looked through his friends' stories. Yes, they experienced jealousy and insecurities, but it wasn't at the scale we have now.

We gain a false sense of understanding through watching things. Watching a cooking video online doesn't mean we can whip up a perfect soufflé, and watching Bob Ross won't make us expert painters. For both of these skills there's work required. That work can be monotonous, repetitive, and frustrating, just like love. Even if we share a bed and a life with the same partner for 50 years, if we never engage in that work we might find ourselves at our 50th anniversary with no more understanding of each other or of love than we had on our first date.

We have to dive into love to really see what it's about. All these expectations and conditions we place on our experiences around love only serve to block the flow of the love surrounding us. Often we hold these beliefs to protect ourselves from getting hurt.

---

[*]   Especially financial

SPOILER ALERT: You can't avoid getting hurt in this game called love.

It's okay that we have some skewed, inaccurate, and outright ludicrous expectations and beliefs around love. It's a challenging idea to wrap our heads around, and when we're not clear on it, it feels like a scavenger hunt both within and around us.

There are so many bootleg versions of love that have been sold to us at a profit—attention, beauty, power, influence, control—but most of these are taking us even further away from realizing love.

The first step is to acknowledge our beliefs around love and to kindly let them go to make room for the simple beauty of what love can really be.

Love doesn't have prerequisites.

Love isn't earned or found, it's realized.

Love is so vast that it can love things that feel unlovable.

Love exists more as an action than a thing.

You are love, I am love, it's all the other mess that needs to get cleaned away for us to really notice this.

To love is to have an open heart, to let go of old ideas of love and make room for more. It requires an open mind, so let's start there.

SPOILER ALERT: YOU CAN'T AVOID GETTING HURT IN THIS GAME CALLED LOVE.

41.

DON'T FALL IN LOVE WITH POTENTIAL

Ogi Ogas and Sai Gaddam are two data scientists who analyzed about a billion Internet searches to investigate what type of porn men and women look for. They blended that information with research from evolutionary biology, sexual psychology, and other sciences to get a picture of what men and women desire.

They found that men searched for more visual types of porn while women searched for more literary forms.[*] These literary representations for women often involve stories of taming the bad boys, the billionaires, the vampires, and the beasts.[**] They describe this as "Taming the Wild Coconut."

"Women want their romance heroes to be like coconuts: hard and tough on the outside, but soft and sweet on the inside. But the hero's sweet interior can't be available to just anyone. Only the heroine gets to crack him open. The hero is granted free rein to be a badass with everyone else, as long as he's tender and attentive with the heroine."

You've probably realized at this point that many of the mistakes we make in love revolve around the fact that our expectations have been shaped by the media. In romance novels and on TV and film, very rarely will a healthy relationship be the central story, because, let's be honest, those would be boring. So instead we're

---

[*]   Instead of watching porn, they want to read it.
[**] Sound familiar?

given over-romanticized stories about situations that sound nice, but would be way more unhealthy in real life; this wild coconut fantasy would be one of them.

Everyone has potential to be better, but unlocking another person's potential is their responsibility, not yours. I get it, we grew up reading *Twilight* and watching *Beauty and the Beast*, and the idea of taming the guy who seems untamable gets exciting. But the goofball you're wasting time over doesn't sparkle in the sun, and living in their mother's basement gives them little room to have dancing teacups and candlesticks.* What these "tame the coconut" fantasies do is just leave us stuck with someone who we think will change, but won't. If anything, they'll change us, and drain us.

I've been guilty of falling for potential, thinking I would be a good influence, and the other person would evolve with me at their side, but that's not love. We're not here to treat others as projects we can nudge, influence, and encourage; we need to love what's in front of us. Loving someone for the version of them you want them to be isn't love, nor is it sustainable; it's just a recipe for heartache and exhaustion. Different people have different experiences, perspectives, and priorities. Let's stop trying to mold them into us—they're not us.

Love doesn't have much room to breathe in a space where there's judgment and loving someone for their potential is just that. It also adds conditions to who they can be in order for them to earn your love. If they decide not to head in that direction, resentment can grow.

Loving someone for who they could be will blind us to who they are. Ignoring red flags because you're wearing rose-colored glasses** is only delaying the inevitable. We are better off entering situations where our needs are clear and we're not worrying if the other person is into us*** or focusing on their potential. Instead, we see them for who they are, accept them,

---

* That's also a fire hazard.
** Waddup, BoJack?
*** Which motivates us to be less authentic.

and decide if they're a good fit for us. This applies to friendships, romantic partnerships, and even working with people.

I understand the excitement of first meeting someone and fantasizing about all the possibilities and potential. It's a lot of fun, but it fizzles away, and then what are we left with?

People do change and have amazing potential, but there's no guarantee that potential will ever be realized. We need to also respect that we don't actually have much power to change other people, nor should we try. Think about your biggest changes in life and how they really only happened when *you* were ready to make them. That same principle applies to others.

If you've been doing the work to better yourself and establish who you are, you shouldn't settle for someone who has done any less. We're getting older every day, and we have to take ownership over the work that needs to be done for self-growth and development. If you come across someone who isn't there yet, that's okay, but realize it's not your job to get them there. It's romantic to think you can be the hero or tame the beast, but those ideas should be left to the corny romance novels they sell at the grocery store.

Let's not allow our unrealistic expectations of other people, how we can change them, or the idea that their potential is closer than it is ruin the wonderful relationships we have. Let's love people for who they are, as much as we can. Trying to make someone anyone they're not will only lead us down a road of bitterness and resentment.

If you want to fall in love with potential, let it be your own.

If you're in the mood to tame a beast, look within, shower it with love, and you'll see how much of your potential[*] you can bring out.

---

[*] And sparkle

LOVING SOMEONE FOR WHO THEY COULD BE WILL BLIND US TO WHO THEY ARE.

42.

LOVE IS FUEL, NOT GLUE

There are no happily ever afters, but there will always be a morning after, when the magic fades and the only thing keeping everything together is the work we do to keep it together. Some call that the end of the honeymoon phase, where we're no longer swooning, super-strong emotions no longer consume us, our eyes wander, and there are petty arguments over who needs to do the dishes.

I've struggled with this—the excitement of adventure and romance have faded and we've fallen into the tomb of routine and monotony. I crave something more, but I know that *more* will also lose its luster in 12 to 18 months.

Dating apps and social media make it feel like we have unlimited options, so why bother to stay with the person we're with; everyone looks happier, has better posture, and would never put banana peels in the recycling bin.[*] Are we doomed to live a life unfulfilled in a situation that doesn't feed our flame?

Often this happens because of our expectations around long-term love. We put our best foot forward during the early days and then fall into autopilot as

---

[*]   I've said too much.

the years go by. What we have to recognize is that **relationships are living things that need to be fed, nurtured, and taken care of for as long as we want them to live.**

Love isn't the glue that keeps us together, it's the fuel that keeps us working at it. Relationships are a journey where you have to pave the path ahead of you, and love is what we tap into to get through the most challenging parts.

No matter the relationship, we're building something with another person, and every day at the construction site won't be the most exciting. The stronger the foundation, the stronger we are as individuals, the more we can hold up. The more we work at it, the more our bonds strengthen over time instead of decaying. **We either grow together or grow apart.**

I want to say a relationship is like a fine wine that gets better with time, mainly because it's a hot line and it rhymes, but it suggests that things will get better by themselves, and all we have to do is sit in a dark basement doing nothing.

If we can acknowledge the honeymoon phase is just that, a phase, we can actively work to use tools and strategies at our disposal to not simply depend on the excitement of the new to keep things going.

Loving someone isn't enough to keep them around; loving someone is enough to work at keeping them around.

Here are a few tips to keep things exciting with your relationships well into your wrinkled years:

1. Share Experiences

The reason relationships are amazing is because we get to share experiences. The reason puppy love is a thing is because we grow up with our partner and have so many "firsts" with them. These shared experiences are a solid foundation and bond to our relationships. We love sharing, it's the reason social media is so popular and why we read Amazon reviews before we buy things.[*]

As life gets busier and more complicated, the opportunities for new experiences to find us are few and far between, and because of that, falling into routine can be a death sentence for the relationship. We won't be starry-eyed teenagers forever, having so many new experiences that we're over the moon with the people we share them with, and we have to take this into our own hands. Plan new experiences, put them in your calendars, and make them a priority. Have a shared bucket list, and recognize the emotional bonds created when we experience new situations together.

This could include taking classes together, trying new restaurants, watching movies, traveling, and even sex. **Feeding the relationship new shared experiences will strengthen what you have between each other.**

2. Don't Test Each Other

She wanted to see if he'd remember her birthday, and he didn't. He wanted her to notice that he wasn't having fun at her friend's party, but she didn't. Be mindful not to put each other on trial to prove love. Having to prove our love or require others to prove their love is a chase for validation, and seeking validation prevents pathways to love. To combat the need for validation and testing our partner's love, we have to communicate our needs much more openly. We

---

[*] Or at least count the stars

have to ensure our partner knows how we feel, and when we feel it. We have to recognize that our partner may not be good at things that come naturally to us, and vice versa, so open communication is essential.

I know it's scary to say how you feel and what you need, we've all experienced shame around sharing needs before. But it's worse thinking about never getting that chance, or exploding because you've kept too much inside, hoping your partner was going to read your mind.

Save the tests for the classroom; be open and clear with the love in your life.

3. Value Your Partner

We know enough about our partner to say the exact things to hurt them where it counts. We can weaponize their secrets, their doubts, and their insecurities, and we often do during heated arguments. Doing this may leave us victorious in the battle, but we're sure going to lose the war, and most likely our partner.

Let's spend more time acknowledging our partner's strengths, and making space for them to be awesome, than tearing them down.

Trying to change our partner and manipulate them into being something they're not will block pathways of love. Ensure you share deep values, have a shared vision of the life you want, and let go of the small stuff.[*]

4. Intentions over Expectations

We expect the world of others and less of ourselves, and make things worse by not communicating those expectations in the first place. Instead of having

---

[*] SPOILER ALERT: There will be a lot of small stuff, and it will feel like big stuff.

expectations, let's set intentions and share them with your partner so they can join you in a common direction you both can head toward. I can't expect my partner to drop everything when I'm having a bad day, especially when I haven't even told them I'm having a bad day. But we can set an intention to have a distraction-free date night once a week, or one hour a day, or something else manageable between the two[*] of you.

Setting intentions isn't about knowing the right direction to head toward, it's about heading forward. Love requires movement and progress, and it's okay if we don't know where we're going; we'll adjust as we go.

5. Sex, Sex, Sex

Our ideas around sex are complex, and are often attributed to how we were raised, combined with culture, religion, and the romantic comedies we see on TV. The easiest way to put it is: **your sex life, much like the rest of your relationship, has to get better over time, not worse.** Better may mean quality over quantity, or sensuality over lust. Whatever it is, there has to be a forward evolution. There needs to be open communication around sex, and it has to be recognized as a shared experience, and less as a gift partners give each other. There can't be any guilt or shame around wanting and not wanting sex, and that safe space has to be established early and honored throughout the relationship. Ensure you and your partner are on the same page when it comes to sex, and make plenty of time for it.

---

[*]   Or three; I don't know how many people are in your relationship.

6. Forgive, Forgive, Forgive

A relationship isn't a chess game; we can't aim to strategically hold power over our partner. We accept them with love and make space for them to make mistakes and have flaws,* knowing they'll do the same for us. Not only does this set the tone for the love we have between each other, it sets the tone for the love we have for ourselves. Forgiveness is key, and we'll explore forgiveness in much more depth later in this book.

There won't be a happily ever after, but there can definitely be a happily continuing to work on it. We tend to treat relationships like most things, a checkbox that doesn't require as much attention once we get it, but with divorce rates so high around the world, that isn't the best attitude to have.

The longer people are together, the deeper the reservoir and the wider the pathways of their love can be, and tapping into those will be the endless source of motivation, enthusiasm, and effort required for the relationship to continue building upon itself. Being in love won't give us the tools to make it work, but being in love will make us work at discovering those tools.

Things can always get better, and things can always get worse; there is no seventh heaven or rock bottom in love. Deep love isn't the outcome of two perfect people being together forever, it's building something sturdy and special over time, despite challenges and flaws. Love isn't the breeze that pushes us across the ocean; it's the awareness that keeps us adjusting the sails.

Don't ever think love is enough to keep people around. It's not some magical Gorilla Glue that will bond your fingers together forever. Instead, it's the fuel we use to power our efforts, attitudes, and energy to make things work.

---

* . . . aka be human.

LOVE ISN'T THE GLUE THAT KEEPS US TOGETHER, IT'S THE FUEL THAT KEEPS US WORKING AT IT.

43.
MIXED SIGNALS MEAN NO

It's one thing to crash a girls' brunch, it's another to offer your opinion on the guy issues they didn't ask you to chime in on.

"Guys are so complicated!" one of the girls proclaimed as her friends agreed. I could see it in their eyes as they relived moments of frustration with the guys in their lives.

I couldn't hide the confusion on my face as I noticed the consensus on all of their faces, and I said something I shouldn't have at that moment.

"Guys aren't complicated, you just complicate them."

At this point I should have run.

Instead, I stood there getting a flurry of stories, accusations, and questions as if I had just signed up to be the representative for all guys on the planet. The questions were more rhetorical, and I could see I had opened a can of worms that wasn't going to close soon, but I'd brought it upon myself. I tried my best to listen and began picking up on one large theme.

Mixed signals + hope = dangerous combination.

"Why would he say he likes me and then not call?"

"Why does he hold my hand in private, but not in public?"

"Why do I get a morning text every day, and then not hear from him for the rest of the day?"

"Why does he make plans with me only to cancel?"

I try to imagine who these guys are, but the only faces I come up with are friends of mine who experience the same things with girls. I mean I've personally asked myself those same questions, but rarely did I conclude the answer was, "because they're complicated." That's because I've also been guilty of doing all of those things as well.

Often the answer that really resonates with me is, "Because they can."

Working as a schoolteacher for a few years taught me that behavior exists when validated. **When we let someone get away with something we don't like, don't be surprised if they do it again.** This isn't to say that all the confusing mixed messages sent by people are meant to hurt us or exploit our feelings. I think often people are confused in their own life and that spills into their actions.

The moment we no longer hold space for this type of behavior to exist, it'll stop, but that may not necessarily be what we want.

I had someone cancel four dates on me after making them. After a little time of confusion, I decided to nip this in the bud and told them we weren't going to try to reschedule again. They were hurt, and said they understood. I took a leap of faith, got vulnerable, and told them it didn't feel good to get canceled on so much and I'd much prefer not to try again to avoid disappointment. They thanked me for my honesty, explained that they were going through stuff and that once they got things in alignment, they would hit me up and try again. I left that window open.

Months went by and I never heard from them again.

The writing was on the wall that despite all that this person SAID, their AC-TIONS told a different story. This doesn't require us to be high-end detectives or psychologists to pick up on subtle nuances and gestures. It just requires us to remember that actions speak much louder than words. That person's actions made it crystal clear that I wasn't a priority, but I HOPED that was wrong. I hoped there was a better explanation that didn't make me feel so bad, so I made excuses and held space for them to do it to me over and over again.

So let's keep it simple, in **the name of self-love and clarity in your life: TAKE MIXED SIGNALS AS A NO.**

See how uncomfortable that felt to read? Yeah, that's why we prefer to live in hopeful ambiguity instead of unpleasant clarity.

How we spend our time is a great indicator of what really matters to us, consciously and unconsciously. The people that matter to you the most will get your time, love, energy, and attention; your calendar shows your priorities more than your words.

There isn't one set of answers to explain why people send mixed signals. They're confused, conflicted, unsure, multitasking, or just scared. It's not easy being open and honest with ourselves, let alone with other people. It's easier to say yes to someone and then cancel on them later than it is to say no from the start. **It's easier to seem nice than it is to actually be nice.** We want to be liked and to have people around, but we can also get uncomfortable if they are too close, so we pull away. None of this means people are intentionally being vague to harm us, it means they're ordinary awkward people, just like us. We can have love and compassion for them, but that can't be more important than the love and compassion we have to show ourselves if their actions are disturbing our peace, which is our pathway to feeling love.

The WHY questions the girls asked are important, but not as important as the question they should be asking themselves: *Why are you putting up with it?*

Accepting mixed signals as a no takes the hope out of the equation and saves us a lot of heartache and confusion. It will also set the tone to other people as to how they can treat us. They can play games with other people, but not us. We can only do this if there isn't fear of losing them, but really, how much of them do we already have?

Guys aren't complicated, and neither are girls, we're just scared, and we're not all the best communicators. Our actions can tell our story better than our words, and when those actions show you something, believe it. Hope is hollow and just delays an uncomfortable reality that's hiding around the corner.

When people send mixed signals, it's less about you, and more about them. They're not serving the needs you have for security, certainty, and assurance; you're allowed to want that. Don't look at these situations as a failure or rejection of yourself. See them as gifts of clarity that help you better define what's right and wrong for you. When a guy or a girl has found their own clarity and love, that can be spread to you. When they haven't, you can still share some with them, but not at the expense of your boundaries, self-love, and self-respect.

This applies beyond romantic relationships. I get mixed signals from people I want to work with and friendships I want to develop. I had to realize the hard way that a *maybe* really was a *no*.

Accept mixed signals as a no until the one sending those signals gets their shit together; if they do, you will have helped them find that clarity. If they don't, then it's another bullet dodged, and lesson learned.

GUYS AREN'T COMPLICATED, AND NEITHER ARE GIRLS, WE'RE JUST SCARED.

44.
INTERDEPENDENT RELATIONSHIPS > CODEPENDENT RELATIONSHIPS

"You complete me!"

Such a romantic thought, but it's actually the epitome of toxic bullshit; that's not what a healthy relationship is. It doesn't matter if we're talking about a spouse, love, parent, child, family member, friend, or even just someone you work with, codependent relationships may look like love, may sound like love, but they're definitely not love.

I'm talking about the "fix me, save me, validate me" relationship; the dramatic, Bobby and Whitney, on-again, off-again type of relationship. A roller-coaster ride makes for some exciting times, but ultimately leaves everyone depleted and worse off than they started. These up-and-down, unpredictable, abusive situations aren't love. These relationships where we compromise who we are and suffocate all we need to receive love aren't love. These intense levels of attachment and dependence are not love.

As Dr. Renee A. Exelbert describes it: "Codependency is a circular relationship in which one person needs the other person, who in turn, needs to be needed. The codependent person, known as 'the giver,' feels worthless unless they are needed by—and making sacrifices for—the enabler, otherwise known as 'the taker.'"

Interdependent relationships, on the other hand, are a balance of self and others within relationships, with both partners working to meet each other's needs in meaningful ways.*

I understand, many of us were taught at a very young age to feel worthy through the acceptance and love from others. We all feel like we're not enough, and we hope that someone loving us will fix this, and we begin to do anything to earn and keep that love; but that's not love, that's toxicity. Many of us have been caught in that cycle our entire lives. Maybe our parents never fully let us grow up and always wanted to ensure we needed them on some level to feel like we matter, so now we play catchup and try to make everyone else happy for the rare moments of their approval and validation. We kill our wishes and desires for others; sometimes it's so bad, we won't even share our wishes with others out of fear of losing them. We fear being honest, we fear being ourselves, we live in constant numbing fear of being abandoned and decide (consciously or subconsciously) to remain in abusive situations, whether verbal, physical, or psychological, because it's better than being alone, and to keep it real, it's familiar, and rhymes with the rest of our life's trauma. We then catch ourselves being both the victim and perpetrator of this toxicity, relying on guilt and shame and other kinds of emotional blackmail to get our way. Everything is fear based, but we put a pretty bow on it and think it's love.

---

* Even simpler put: codependence is you and your dog, while interdependence is you and your cat. Unless your cat is a weirdo.

This is not love, this is trauma bonding, codependency, polluted bullshit, and today's the day that cycle gets broken.

We don't complete anybody, and nobody completes us. **Real love means respecting each other's separateness.** It's learning about the other person, and having them learn about you, it's seeing them and feeling seen, it's holding space for them in your life and having them do the same. We don't own each other, we're not entitled to shit, and we don't need each other like oxygen, that shit sounds hot in an R&B song, but it's deadly to your mind, body, spirit, and ability to actually experience love.

Real love is realized when each person is doing the work to meet and communicate their own needs. It's no one else's job to read our minds and make us happy or feel good about ourselves. **When we have an overflow of that happiness, we can spread it, share it, and receive it from others, but in no way is it our responsibility to be the sole source of love to anyone else on this planet.** We can have a bond, but be independent. This is called interdependence, which is the foundation of interdependent relationships. Interdependent relationships require everyone to be independent but allows space for them to develop closeness, be concerned about the other, and even depend on each other, but none of it involves having to control or be controlled just for people to feel okay. We have to develop our self-worth ourselves, rather than getting it from the other person. We have to learn how to listen to the other without feeling guilty or getting defensive; we have to learn to say NO without guilt.

Relationships grounded in love are based on freedom, accountability, and peace.

This isn't a pipe dream; healthy relationships are possible, and we deserve them. This starts by recognizing the unhealthy and self-destructive relationships in our life. Those are hard, because many of them come with years of history. Oftentimes we gravitate toward relationships that remind us of the ones we experienced in childhood, regardless of whether those relationships were any good for us. It's exciting to win over that guy who seems so emotionally distant 95 percent of the time, because that magical 5 percent feels so good, but that's just like playing slots, hoping the thrill of lining up all those sevens makes up for all that you put in. It's very validating that she gets jealous and demands more of your attention, but it'll never be enough, and all your efforts to reassure her of her worth will be in vain; you can't externally fix what needs attention from within.

The people who bring these toxic situations into our life aren't evil, they just lack the tools and haven't done the work to incorporate the trauma they've experienced. They didn't buy this book, they didn't open themselves up to an idea that love can be better than what they had growing up, and for that, we can have compassion for them. But no fucking way are we going back to that shit. **Stand up for yourself like you would stand up for someone you love,** because the antidote to all this toxicity is opening real paths to love, and that starts with you.

Recognize when you bring that toxic bullshit to yourself and begin to turn the tide into something cleaner and fresher. Realize you'll never find any love and peace being anything besides yourself, and there's no honor in being a martyr to keep others happy. Today is the day we no longer look to others to make us feel worthy, whole, or complete. Today's the day we begin to realize we've always been complete, and therefore worthy and whole, and we should act like it.

STAND UP FOR YOURSELF LIKE YOU WOULD STAND UP FOR SOMEONE YOU LOVE.

45.

THE CURE
FOR LONELINESS

At the time this book is being written, I am living in a large loft space, high ceilings, dozens of windows, and a corner unit so we can get away with making as much noise as we want without disturbing the neighbors.[*] People are always coming over, and there's plenty of room for everyone, but the moment the last guest leaves and I lock the door, my heart sinks.

I'm overcome with a profound sadness and deep emptiness instantly; I'm lonely. After years of being a nomad, sleeping on couches and guest beds, I always thought living on my own, having my own space, and controlling my environment would be so liberating and the solitude so peaceful, but instead, it starts to feel like I'm trapped in an oversized prison, desperate for anyone to come save me from the torture of being in my own company.

For a while I thought the antidote was to make more friends and to pressure my existing friends to come over more often. As long as someone was here, I wouldn't have to hear the deafening silence of my space and the unpleasant thoughts in my head, but it never lasted. They served as temporary relief, and once they left, I'd be stuck with the lonely dread, and a messy apartment to

---

[*]   Unless you count that double-Dutch tournament we thought was wise at 3 A.M. on a Sunday night.

clean up. A million followers on social media don't make me feel less lonely, knowing famous people doesn't make me feel less lonely, nor does getting invited to a lot of fun parties.

I also figured I should meet more girls for casual hookups, put myself out there more. I didn't realize that the more I did that, the more I would want to do it. It was fun and delicious, but not very nutritious. **No matter how many girls I met and had fun with, I was always left wanting more.** There had to be a better way.

Even among quiet and proud introverts, as challenging as it is to be around people, it can be just as hard being alone; we become lonely loners, trying to figure out the perfect balance of desiring our solitude while curing our loneliness.

As a species, we need other people. Loneliness is bad for our health. Research has linked social isolation and loneliness to higher risks for many physical and mental conditions: high blood pressure, heart disease, a weakened immune system, anxiety, depression, cognitive decline, Alzheimer's disease, and even death. Yes, you can die of loneliness.

Being lonely isn't about having or not having people around, it's about the quality of the relationships we have with others. That's why we can be in a room full of people and feel even more isolated, especially if we don't feel known, understood, or cared for deeply by any of those people; that's closeness. To cure loneliness, we have to prioritize the closeness we have with others instead of just trying to find more people to be around.

Before we sit down to watch a movie or take a flight, Lilly asks me if we should wait to get started so I can take an anxiety trip to the bathroom. She knows me well enough that before we're in any situation where we'll be sitting for long, she knows I run to the bathroom in hopes that I won't have to get up again. The simple fact that she recognizes that in me shows me that she both understands and cares about me, which makes me feel seen, closer to her, and much less alone.

We all crave that level of closeness, we want to feel understood and accepted for who we authentically are. We want others to see life in our skin, walk in our shoes, see through our eyes.

As Portia de Rossi so wonderfully put it: "It's good to be loved, it's profound to be understood."

So closeness, feeling understood, and being cared for is a great cure for loneliness, but that doesn't explain how to go about achieving this closeness. We can't necessarily control who will care about us or who will still want to be around us once they see who we really are. So instead of focusing on finding people to understand us, let's focus on understanding others.

Showing more understanding and making a greater effort to care for others will also make us feel less lonely. This can be achieved through wisdom.

Dilip V. Jeste, professor of psychiatry and neurosciences at the UC San Diego School of Medicine, found that wisdom contains six measurable components:

1. Empathy
2. Compassion
3. Self-reflection
4. Emotional regulation
5. Altruism
6. Sense of fairness

All of these components are "prosocial behaviors," meaning they benefit others. Focusing on these prosocial components of wisdom serves to reduce and even prevent loneliness. The more we focus on these behaviors, the wiser we become. The more closeness we create with others, the less lonely we'll feel.

I wasn't doing much of this when I was chasing random girls or inviting as many people as possible over to my place. I was just slapping a bandage on the lonely wound and wondering why I still felt the pain once everyone left.

Prioritizing others, understanding them through THEIR perspective, seeing them as they see themselves, and letting them know you want to care about that real version of them will serve to create a deeper connection with them, and further open a pathway of love between you. This isn't an easy task, it takes work, and there will be times when it feels one-sided, but none of that means it isn't worth pursuing; our well-being is on the line.

I'm not promising you can achieve closeness with that one person you desire, but I am promising that you can create quality relationships with many people and prioritize that quality over quantity.

While we're talking about the quantity of friendships, let's talk about how social media only feeds loneliness. Social media does little to encourage people to be their true selves, so it doesn't serve to help us understand others, or to have others better understand us. **Social media keeps us in touch, but not connected.** Spend enough time scrolling through your phone and you'll feel more lonely, insecure, and in competition with and envious of others; these are all the opposite of the compassion and empathy needed to build closeness. It doesn't matter how many friends you have following you, what matters is how many of those friends know and care about the real you; that version of yourself rarely gets a chance to be shown on these social platforms.

The quality of friendships is much more valuable than quantity. How many people do you have closeness with now? Focus on one person and dedicate time to better knowing who they really are and communicating that you both understand and care for that person. This may be a friend, a partner, or a family member. Quality over quantity matters.

Finding our own purpose is also great for curing loneliness. It's making the effort to better understand ourselves and caring about what we find. Cultivate your own interests, even if you have to do it alone.* Doing things we enjoy will also help us enjoy our own company.

Sometimes the media we consume feeds our loneliness too. The news makes us feel isolated, certain shock-value content that steals our attention leaves us drained after. Finding art that's optimistic, happy, and feel-good will do wonders to improve the feelings we have about ourselves, others, and the world around us.

Lastly, get involved and serve, whether that's getting a puppy you'll be accountable to or fostering communities around things you care about. That might be a bowling league, a book club, helping those in need, or attending comic book conventions. Finding others who get your quirks and actively participating in those communities will also serve to reduce the feelings of loneliness we experience.

I've learned that the work of addressing my loneliness starts with me. **If I don't connect with others, then I can't feel bad that others won't connect with me.** It doesn't matter if I'm famous, easy on the eyes, or have a fun place to party; closeness has to be the priority. As I focus on building a stronger, more authentic relationship with myself, it gets a bit easier to do the same with others, and not worry about getting anything in return. As I practice, I have been feeling less lonely, and more connected.

This hasn't been easy, but it's been completely worth it.

---

* Remember, *alone* isn't the same as *lonely*; we all need solo space.

IF I DON'T CONNECT WITH OTHERS, THEN I CAN'T FEEL BAD THAT OTHERS WON'T CONNECT WITH ME.

46.

LOVE IS
A GOOD FIGHT

Negativity weighs more than positivity. A kind comment won't erase a hurtful one, so if we want harmony with people, we should have way more positive things to counter the negative. And when I say way more, I mean like 20 positive interactions for every one negative reaction. We know coexisting with someone is going to lead to conflict every now and then, but we have to make sure there's more peace than conflict. This 20:1 ratio is something we should consider on a regular day; when it comes to having fights and disagreements, that ratio has to be adjusted.

Now, if there's a conflict, words sting even harder, and we'll have to change that ratio to maybe 30 positive words for every negative. If you need to have an important conversation with someone you care about and you know it may get challenging, you're going to have to be extra mindful of the kindness you put out there. Sharing a problem with someone doesn't mean we have to be jerks about it. Giving a person our attention and being polite and gracious can all go a long way toward ensuring something challenging doesn't get worse.

I used to fall for the trap of hyperbolism[*] when I got into arguments in my past relationships. When things got heated, I would start to question the entire relationship instead of the issue at hand. I thought if we loved each other, we shouldn't fight, and now I realize it needs to be the opposite.

In relationships, there needs to be long periods of peace, but every so often there needs to be a good fight. There's a difference between a good fight and a toxic one, and the passionate romances we see in the media have people thinking certain toxic situations are beautiful; they're not. When communication starts to fizzle, things go off topic, or, even worse, things are left unaddressed, that only feeds anxiety in a relationship. That anxiety grows and eventually erodes a relationship.

A good fight happens within boundaries and serves to open the relationship up. There can be emotion, but there's also space, and there can be tension and friction, but there's an understanding that love still has a spot in the room. We need these good fights to evolve as individuals and as a unit in our relationships.

Thoughts and emotions build up and need to be released because when unaddressed, they can cause bigger problems later. We need a partner who challenges us, wrestles with us, and points out how we're whack, and how we can be better. They are our partner, after all, and they have a front-row seat to us, and care about us enough to notice things that matter. That doesn't mean everything they say will be right, but some of it will be and is worth listening to. If we have a loving partner, even when they don't sound like it, they're saying these potentially unkind things for both of your benefits.

---

[*] Aka drama queening

Again, these unkind things need to be in a healthy ratio to the kind things, and the kind things don't need to be a list either. Kindness can come in the form of various cues: eye contact, turning your body toward the other, putting the phone away, and making efforts to actively listen.[*]

On the other side of the coin, as convenient as it sounds to have a partner who never picks a fight with you, that lack of tension will cause atrophy and harm the growth of the relationship. We all need to grow and get stronger, individually and as a unit, and that requires friction and tension. Too much of it is drama and toxic, not enough of it will break the ties you're trying to form. There has to be a sweet spot.

I've been overly critical and overly criticized in relationships and it sucks being on both ends of it. We're going to eventually hit a bump in the road, and that's not a sign of failure in the relationship, it's a necessary part of it. Let's just ensure it's surrounded by love, kindness, and attention during those wonderful periods of peace.

---

[*]   There's a whole chapter on that in here.

A GOOD FIGHT HAPPENS WITHIN BOUNDARIES AND SERVES TO OPEN THE RELATIONSHIP UP.

47.

LOVE NEEDS TO BE RECEIVED

I know I've been the villain in the stories of others' lives. Beautiful individuals who tried their best to connect with me, overlooking my red flags and being hopeful for my potential while ignoring my intense energy. Back then I thought I was being passive about not being into them the way they were into me. Over time, I realized it was more than that: I wasn't capable of accepting what they wanted to give me.

For me personally, my biggest challenge is not finding love, it's receiving it. So much love exists around me, yet I was closed off to it, and then I'd feel like I lacked love. I get messages daily from people showing me love and I have people in my life that give me love in abundance, but none of that matters if I'm not open to receiving it.

We struggle with accepting compliments, we feel like frauds and failures, and no matter what the rest of the world is telling and showing us, none of it matters if we don't feel like we deserve love.

Sometimes I can't receive the love because I don't feel I can reciprocate; because of that I'm flooded with guilt and feelings of unworthiness. So I decided that if I can't give it back, I shouldn't get it.

Sometimes I feel like the people showing me love don't know the real me, and if they were to discover who I really am, they would reject me, so why bother accepting something that's going to get taken away eventually?

Sometimes I think about those who have rejected me and decide that they're the better measure of who I am. I find myself reading one negative comment online and ignoring the 99 positive ones.

Sometimes receiving love requires me to be vulnerable beyond what I'm comfortable or familiar with, and that's just scary.

Sometimes a voice in my head warns me, "Don't let this go to your head, you ain't shit."[*] In some cases it feels like accepting love will rob me of my independence, and bind me into a contract of expectations I didn't agree to. This happens most in situations where communication isn't the strongest between the other person and myself.

Sometimes it's just overwhelming and I can't explain it. Regardless of being aware that I'm blocking my own blessings, I still go out and search for more love, often chasing affection in all the wrong places.

There isn't a button to open the garage door of our hearts, these moats and walls exist for a reason, and it will take time to unpack those reasons, and then slowly and painfully practice our asses out of the stale mindsets that isolated us from everyone else.

It starts with communication, both inwardly and outwardly. The truth is, I'm not an imposter, I'm here for a reason, you're reading my book for a reason, and there's nothing wrong with me owning and even celebrating that. I'm not giving cooking advice, I'm not building rockets to the moon, I'm not teaching you how to dance. I'm doing what I do best—I put words together in ways to make heavy ideas feel a little bit lighter, that's it, and I'm allowed to accept that people find value in that and appreciate me for it. Just like I appreciate my favorite authors

---

[*] I had a few friends who would say that to me in real life, thinking they were keeping me grounded, but really they were doing more damage than helping.

and musicians and plumbers and mechanics. They add value to my life, and I can honor them with money and by leaving them kind reviews online. We all worked hard to get to where we are, and even if none of the success and accolades will rid us of our insecurities, that shouldn't close us off to love either.

Communicating these ideas to myself regularly is important; it can't be a one-time thing. I have to remind myself that I do important work, and although the best way to measure it is in how it impacts me, there's a lot to learn from paying attention to how it impacts others.

A great way to accept love is to see what a person who loves you sees. This will require some more communication. When I was struggling financially early on in this journey, I told the person I was with that they would be better off with someone more financially stable. Her reply was, "You're kind to me, you're kind to your family, you're kind to my family, and you work hard. That's all that matters to me." Knowing how she saw me and why she loved me allowed me to double down on what mattered to her, and also not worry so much about the other stuff that I thought was important.

I was warned as my fame grew to not let it go to my head, and I thought that meant to reject all love and praise that came my way. I now know it's the opposite, I should receive it graciously, give it generously, and just be mindful of why it's happening. I understand that my work has helped a lot of people, but I also understand that it's simply a distraction for a larger group, and I should be happy I can help in any way I can, and not take this too seriously.

I also found myself belittling those who love me, because "something must be wrong with them if they love me," realizing that my insecurities were serving as the barriers to block the flow of love in my life. This had me chasing people whose love I wasn't receiving, thinking I was only worthy of love if I could win them over. This wasn't just pretty girls, it was the super-famous, high-power players in the industry, and family members who were hyperjudgmental. It felt like acceptance from the most elusive individuals would somehow be worth more than from the people who currently appreciated my existence. I would win some and lose some, but nothing really changed, until I started to own that I was the issue and that accepting that I was worthy of love was more important than winning a specific person over. The truth is, winning them over would have put them in the "something must be wrong with them if they think I'm worthy" category anyway.

The drawbridge can only be lowered from inside our castle; it doesn't matter how much love is surrounding us if it's closed. Accepting and receiving love is a skill that needs to be practiced and expressed out loud.

Now I actively accept compliments with a "Thank you, I receive your kind words." Even before I was a public figure, I was already flooded with such beauty and love from the people that matter most in my life.

It's not just compliments, it's gratitude toward my friends who are regularly calling and checking in on me,[*] and appreciating the ones who get back to me when I reach out to them.

Knowing and communicating our needs is important. We have to teach others how to love us, because if they're doing it in other ways, we may not notice or feel it. Be a little selfish and show others how you want to be loved so they can love you accordingly. This will help us avoid feeling like we're giving and giving and getting nothing in return.

We can't win 'em all, but that doesn't mean we should lose the ones we have. When we don't make efforts to receive the love that exists within and around us, we waste more energy chasing mirages of love in the far-off distances, only to be left thirstier when we get there.

> *"There is a secret about human love that is commonly overlooked: Receiving it is much more scary and threatening than giving it."*
> —John Welwood

---

[*] I see you, Keith Rice.

A GREAT WAY
TO ACCEPT LOVE
IS TO SEE WHAT
A PERSON WHO
LOVES YOU SEES.

48.
LOVE IS ABOUT SETTING INTENTIONS, NOT EXPECTATIONS

The quickest way to be disappointed is to have a lot of expectations.[*] Obviously, having no expectations will lead to no disappointments, but that's not realistic. Having fewer expectations will lead to fewer disappointments, but that might not be enough either.

The moment we set expectations, we've set a trap. Once an expectation is birthed around those we love, we're also setting a subtle fear of them being broken. On top of that, expectations don't really promote one of love's greatest expressions, gratitude. Often it's challenging for anyone to appreciate us for living up to expectations, and things are only noticed when we don't.

Having expectations of others robs us of peace, and it's not fair. We can all relate to times we've felt crushed under the pressure of living up to the expectations of others, whether that be a partner, a parent, friends, or society as a whole, so why continue the cycle?

---

[*]   Hello, final season of *Game of Thrones*!

Expectations often get mistaken for truths and are simplified to either a yes or a no, when life and people are much more complex than that. If I expect you to have my back, I'm also assuming you know every single situation and way you'll need to have my back. Does having my back mean you defend me in a fight, but also take my side when we're picking a place to eat? **Setting expectations is denying nuance, complexity, and the real truths that life holds.** No one is a mind reader, no one is perfect, and it's unfair to hold someone to unrealistic standards.

If you want to have expectations, have them for yourself, and see how many you can live up to while also paying attention to your reaction when you don't live up to your own expectations. Very quickly you'll realize that you can't keep up with your own expectations and it's completely unfair to put them on others.

Now, I'm not promoting relationships free of boundaries, respect, and under-standing; every kite needs its string. We should set boundaries, but respect them as fluid, and ensure they have space for people to find freedom within their lane. We don't complain about stopping at red lights even though it restricts our movements because we see the importance of the boundary. With boundaries in relationships, having them malleable and ensuring commu-nication will do wonders for the quality of that relationship, and make plenty of room for love to breathe.

Expectations are set to chase a specific outcome; it's hoping that some-thing will happen, and being afraid it may not, and being stressed out when it doesn't. Instead of expectations, let's focus on setting intentions with those who we care about the most. Expectations are what we NEED to happen; intentions are aiming for what we want to happen. Interestingly enough, the word *intention* can also be defined as "the healing process of a wound."

Intentions allow us to detach from outcomes, and instead give structure and direction to our energy.

Expectation: *My partner should anticipate my needs.*
Intention: *I will ask for what I want clearly.*
Expectation: *My partner will be faithful to me.*
Intention: *Let's work on this relationship in such a way that we don't cross intimate boundaries with other people outside of us.*

Intentions aren't one-off rules and declarations, they're something we have to remain mindful of all the time. Often we set expectations to be what we think will help our intentions, but really the intentions are all we need.

Yes, I know the famous quote, "The road to hell is paved with good intentions," so let me add to that, "but the road to heaven becomes clear when you're intentional with your choices."

If we want to experience more love in our life, we have to be mindful of our energy, and how we impact those we care about the most. If we love someone, the last thing we want to do is drown them in rules and expectations. Instead, we can share with them our boundaries and intentions, and they can set expectations for themselves to have freedom within those lanes.

Please don't twist this chapter to be an excuse to be a free-loving fuckboy who doesn't have to stay committed to your partner, especially if you know your partner has boundaries. Part of being in a relationship is to honor and protect both of your boundaries but to recognize that those boundaries have to work for both of you. The boundary between the beach and water changes, so does the boundary between day and night. It's a constant negotiation, but the constant part is what will promote the growth and strengthen your bond.

Parents, this goes for you too. Set intentions with your children instead of strict expectations. Expecting your child to be a doctor/lawyer/engineer will cause you both more stress than any of you need. Set intentions that you want them to be self-sufficient, contributing members of society and increasingly promote freedom for them within that intention. They're growing up in a time much different than yours; respect that, love them, and watch them flourish with your love.

IF YOU WANT TO HAVE EXPECTATIONS, HAVE THEM FOR YOURSELF, AND SEE HOW MANY YOU CAN LIVE UP TO.

49.

LOVE WITH YOUR EYES OPEN

I get to the sushi spot just in time, then after waiting 10 minutes, I text her, "I'm at the table in the back corner of the restaurant." She immediately calls. "I'm sorry, I wish you'd confirmed, I'm at a work meeting, I'm so sorry, I feel horrible, I'll make this up to you."

I get it, mistakes happen, but this was the third time this "mistake" had happened, and this time, she also subtly blamed me.

After a few hours, and a long session of breathing, I sent a voice note: "Hey, with all love and respect, don't worry about making it up, this has happened before, and it doesn't feel good. I know you didn't mean it maliciously, but you also put it on me to remind you of plans we made together. I enjoy spending time with you, but this isn't behavior I want to get used to. I wish you all the best."

We can love someone and not have to blind ourselves to their flaws. This over-romanticized idea of love that we see in the movies sets the bar for un-conditional love, and if we don't have that, we think something must be wrong. Back on Earth, after the credits roll, the real world has real problems. Everyone we love, including ourselves, will have shortcomings, room for improvement, and outright moments of wackness. None of that disqualifies us from the experience of love, but all of that is reason for us to love with our eyes open.

We don't have to enable anyone's flaws in order to love them. We can love a family member who's bad with money and just not lend them money. We can love someone who struggles with addiction but honor our own boundaries not to participate in it. We can love somebody who thinks mint–chocolate chip ice cream is delicious, or somebody who doesn't believe *Die Hard* isn't a Christmas film. We can love somebody who doesn't take care of their health or who hijacks every conversation and makes it about themselves.

To love with our eyes open is to be able to acknowledge the human in everyone and still direct the love we have their way. If those people guilt us for not validating their bullshit, then we can love ourselves a bit more and strengthen the boundaries so as not to get caught up in things that will only reduce that flow of love. I know my own flaws and shortcomings, but I'm still going to be kind to myself. Being kind to myself doesn't mean giving in to my vices, it means being loving, open, and understanding when I make mistakes and encouraging an environment for me to do and be better.

Many of us grew up looking up to our parents, flaws and all, and many of those flaws present themselves in the people and partners we choose to be around; that's no accident, but it's not necessarily a wise move. We can hold space for people to figure themselves out and be better, but let's not be blind to the fact that some people aren't willing or ready to start that journey. We must be okay with backing off in order to maintain our levels of love, energy, and peace.

I don't need someone to be perfect to love them, and I don't need to be perfect to be loved, but that doesn't mean we can't be aware of the areas of improvement, so these experiences of love don't descend into a place where love becomes increasingly hard to realize.

I know it's not easy to have boundaries with the people we care about the most, but if we really care about them those boundaries are necessary. Taking care of your needs makes you available and pleasant to be around when you are with others.

You're not a hero for sticking around after it's clear you should leave, and you're not a selfish monster for walking away from something that no longer serves you. Love requires an open heart and thrives with open eyes.

Love isn't blind, but it can be shortsighted.

LOVE ISN'T BLIND, BUT IT CAN BE SHORTSIGHTED.

50.
LOVE IS EXPLAINING AND ACCEPTING YOUR FLAWS

Throughout this book there are reminders that you don't have to be perfect or "enough" to share and experience love, and a great way to reinforce this is by accepting and learning how to explain your imperfections to those that matter to you the most. So here goes:

I get moody when I'm hungry and I'm a straight talker, so I can often sound rude. I don't avoid conflict, and if I'm excited, I can lose my focus and interrupt people. I don't enjoy opening up to others, and I can view relationships as a threat to my independence and identity. When I'm overwhelmed, I'm not the greatest at expressing it to others, and I sometimes assume people should just be able to read my mind. I've been burned in past relationships, both romantic and business, so I'm very sensitive to people whose words don't match their actions, and I hold grudges forever. **Even though I want depth in my relationships, I deny it by refusing to be vulnerable.** I think Scorpios romanticize their toxic behaviors and I resent specific Scorpios for it. I'm not the most organized, and I snore.

Okay, your turn.

This may not be first date talk, but these are things it's better to reveal consciously and intentionally instead of through your actions over time. I know it's scary showing your flaws and scars, but they're going to come out anyways. We can't put makeup and filters on our personalities forever. **If meaningful relationships with other people is the goal, then sharing our imperfections is essential.**

To be in a healthy relationship is to be a teacher and a student. Teach the other person about who you are, what your needs are, and how you should be treated, and be a curious student about the person you're with. This reduces miscommunication and conflicts and empowers everyone to contribute to the harmony of the relationship.

I am flawed, you are flawed, I will cause trouble, you will cause trouble; let's teach each other how, so we're better prepared to deal with it when it comes. That may mean keeping a granola bar in your purse, not holding it against me if I'm unresponsive for half a day, and lying to me about when your birthday is if you were born between October 23 and November 21.

Teaching me that horror movies trigger you or that you don't enjoy certain foods or textures or that conflicts bring up childhood trauma will better equip me to understand and serve you in the way that's best for you. Knowing your flaws is just as important as knowing your food allergies, and if we want love in the room, we'll accept them instead of judging them.

I know it's scary to bare ourselves to someone else. We fear rejection, we want them to like us, so sharing anything about us that is less than perfect will send them running the other way, right?

Well, everyone wants to have an ideal partner, but "ideal" is not someone with clear skin, a flat tummy, and farts that smell like vanilla. An ideal partner is someone who meets your needs, but if you were actually perfect, you wouldn't have any needs. Since we're all imperfect, let's share that with others so they can love us accordingly, and let's encourage them to share that with us, so we can love them the same.

Pro tip: When you do unexpectedly encounter a flaw in another person, address it at the level of the flaw, not the whole relationship. **Everything is not make or break for a relationship when a smaller, simpler fix can be an option.** Don't dump me because I snore, maybe we can get earplugs, separate beds, or I can buy a CPAP machine, or you can learn to find it adorable.

We all love people who are far from perfect, and the love we give them is far from perfect. That's okay. The more we love someone, the more they fit us just as they are. The most we can see anyone we love is CLOSE to perfect, so let's love them close to perfect.

This is a choice we can make for relationships we want to last beyond the short term, where who we really are, scars and flaws and all, will be revealed whether we want them to be or not. Let's connect those imperfections to our needs and encourage our partner to do the same so we can open the flow of love between each other even wider, serve the other the way they need, and teach them how to be there for us the way we want.

> *"Nobody's perfect, but you're perfect for me."*
> — Missy Elliott

EVERYTHING IS NOT MAKE OR BREAK FOR A RELATIONSHIP WHEN A SMALLER, SIMPLER FIX CAN BE AN OPTION.

51.

RELATIONSHIPS WE BUILD > RELATIONSHIPS WE HAVE

If you strongly believe in soulmates, you should probably skip this chapter.

I'm the child of an arranged marriage. My parents met at their wedding and have been together ever since. About 10 years ago, two of my cousins, both younger than me, went to Punjab to attend their older brother's wedding, and ended up being introduced to girls and getting married that same week.[*] As of today, those three brothers are the only nondivorced relatives I have on my mother's side of the family.

A collection of 43 different studies involving over 11,000 couples spanning 20 years concluded that the setup and maintenance of our relationships matter more than the personalities of the individuals in them. This means to create a healthy relationship we have to work on the relationship more than relying on compatibility. The life we create with our partner is more important than trying to find a specific partner that fits the life we already have.

---

[*]   My aunt is a hall-of-famer for making that happen.

That takes work, but the work is worth it.

This explains why arranged marriages can be successful: both partners share a common priority when they enter into it, whether that is family, tradition, culture, or something else. I'm not going to jump into the debate on whether an arranged marriage is better than a romantic marriage, but the qualities of it that work should be noted.

Having healthy romantic relationships is probably the most important thing we can do during this life to enjoy it, and the mysteries of doing so seem to only grow as time goes on. How do we find that right person, how do we become the right person, and why do so many other couples seem happier than us?

It's never healthy to compare, especially when you can't see fully what's actually happening with other people. Instead of looking for a perfect partner, or trying to change the one you have, the priority needs to be building a great relationship.

We have to set up conditions that will allow our relationships to flourish, instead of setting up expectations of our partner that they can never meet. This means focusing on shared norms, inside jokes, and shared experiences more than just hoping the other person will "get" you.

This doesn't take away from the importance of what individuals bring to the table in a relationship. Who you are and what you're going through will impact the quality of relationships you have, both romantic and platonic.

According to the study published by the National Academy of Sciences, as individuals,

- your life satisfaction
- your physical state (are you distressed, irritable)
- your emotional state
- your attachment anxiety
- your attachment avoidance

will all play a big role in the success of your relationships.

What will play an even bigger role in determining the success of your romantic relationship is:

- your perceived partner commitment.
- your appreciation.
- your sexual satisfaction.
- your perceived partner satisfaction.
- the amount of conflict.

When we focus on the personality of our relationship, we can zoom out and make decisions more holistically, instead of being nitpicky, petty, and resentful, just because as individuals we have so many differences.

This doesn't just apply to romantic relationships. Some of my closest friends are people I now have very little in common with, but we've had healthy friendships that have spanned decades because the dynamic of the relationship works. Although we are different, there is harmony because we don't see each other often, we give each other space, we have little or no expectations of each other, and we share a lot of norms and experiences from over the years.

The dynamic of the relationship keeps us around each other more than the things we have in common. So although they may make choices I don't agree with, I can still enjoy them. Maybe we make it clear not to get in business together, or not to share too many personal secrets, or just to see each other once a month.

We're not just IN relationships, we're building and designing them.

We need to design our relationships for success, we need to design our marriages so we're not part of the high divorce rate. Much of this depends on abandoning old scripts and traditions that dictate how these things are *supposed* to work.

We are unique individuals with unique needs, and we connect with other unique individuals, but then try to cram ourselves into a traditional partnership that has roots in times before electricity. The pressures of those traditions weigh on us and make it hard to build a relationship together. Couples go broke throwing lavish weddings and crumble as a unit because of financial stress. The gap between how a relationship should be and what it is starts to widen, and we start to think we're with the wrong person when really we've just been approaching things the wrong way.

Loving someone will never be enough to make things work, but loving someone will be enough to work on things. Building a solid foundation on things that matter will lead to a more successful relationship than simply being with someone because they tick off boxes. That's going to present a challenge to people who are currently looking for life partners on apps with preset standards of who a person needs to be. A blank slate, an open mind, and an open heart would probably end up being much more effective.

When building together, we can look at each person in the relationship as a pillar, and the more space between the pillars, the more it can hold up. Let's stop romanticizing jealousy, ownership, and high doses of each other and celebrate two independent people working together to build something bigger than themselves.

As I said in the beginning, this isn't for the devout believers in soulmates, it's for people who want to reassume control over what their relationships are and where they want to take them.

WE'RE NOT JUST IN RELATIONSHIPS, WE'RE BUILDING AND DESIGNING THEM.

52.
LISTENING IS LOVE

After she signed for her new apartment, she came over and showed me a carefully drawn diagram on her phone of how she was going to lay out her furniture. She was excited; it was her first place of her own. She had done the measurements, found affordable furniture, and now it was time to share that with me.

Of course the first thing I did was criticize the fact that she was going to put a rug by the couch. She had just gotten a puppy, so the last thing she should do is have a rug before the puppy was fully house-trained, right?

The enthusiasm drained from her eyes. She put her phone away and said, "I didn't ask you whether I should put down a rug, I just wanted to share something I was excited about."

That conversation became the catalyst for our eventual breakup.

I'm a shitty listener. I'm a debater, so I listen closely, but only to find holes in an argument. I listen to what people say, but I rarely hear them.[*] Since taking a deeper dive into the idea of listening, I've become more aware of how often I cut other people off or stay quiet waiting for my turn to talk, but not absorbing what they say.

---

[*] Know the difference!

We've all complained about not being heard, but rarely do we call ourselves out for not listening. Because I'm not listening as well as I should, I'm not making the connections with others the way I want. Those connections are really important, especially with those we care about.

To love is to understand. To understand is to listen.

In a world of constant distractions, listening is one of the valuable things we can do to show others how important they are to us. Listening is an art, it's a skill, and most important, it's an act that opens pathways to love.

This is profound but not rocket science. Everyone feels great around a generous listener; it feels amazing when you feel heard, because you know you're seen and you matter. When we connect on that level we feel safe, and can further grow.

Listening heals. It creates space and shares your presence. **Our presence is one of the most important gifts we can give anyone.** Generous listening allows us to experience empathy on an abundant level. When we're really there listening to someone we get the clearest moment of what it actually feels like to be them, good or bad. The more we listen to someone, the more we'll understand them. The more we understand them, the less we'll judge them; that's the empathy we all want.

Being a better listener to others will make us better listeners toward ourselves.

Listening to ourselves will make us more self-aware about how we speak to ourselves.

Listening to ourselves will help reveal our deepest truths.

With all this said, to realize more love in our life, we have to shut the fuck up and listen much more than we currently do.

Having ears means we CAN listen, but it doesn't mean we DO listen. As I said earlier, it's not only an act of love, it's a skill and art that requires mindfulness and practice. I'm a shitty listener,[*] and I realize that much of it has to do with my focus, priorities, and agenda when communicating with others. Love won't make us better listeners, but love can inspire us to work harder at becoming better listeners.

Here are a few tips to becoming a more generous listener:

1. Listen with Your WHOLE Existence

Put the phone away, cut out the distractions, turn your body toward the person, and make them everything in that moment. To really listen to someone is to meditate on them. There is no past or future, there's just now, and in the now is the person in front of you, and what they're saying is all that matters.

You may lose focus while they speak; that's okay, be aware of it, catch yourself, and gently bring your focus back onto them. **To listen is to receive, not respond. Be there for them.**

2. Listen to Learn, Not to Be Polite

We don't become better listeners by focusing on listening to only certain people. We become better listeners by actively listening to everyone. Sometimes these people aren't interesting, they overwhelm us with information, or they say things that are hard to hear.[**] We have to be mindful of the challenges when it comes to listening to others and make adjustments to improve on them. The simplest step is to set out the goal to learn something from every conversation. Doing so shifts the focus from what you're going to say and instead prioritizes what you're learning.

---

[*]   Yes, I'm assuming you're a shitty listener too; whether you admit it or not, we can all be better.
[**]   Like talking about politics.

3. Acknowledge Your Agenda, Then Tell It to Shut Up

If we're not listening to be polite, we're often listening just waiting for our turn to speak. Sometimes it's selfish, other times the person says something that triggers an emotion, or memory, or counterpoint and we want to respond to it. Sometimes we even cut the person off, because otherwise we'll forget the point we wanted to make; this needs to be addressed. **The purpose of really listening is not to respond, find holes in their points, or one-up their cool story; it's to learn.** In order to do that, we have to become more aware of when we're emotionally triggered by the things people say. It may not even be a bad emotion, you may have a relevant idea to contribute to the conversation, but that's not the point; the point is to listen.

For this to happen we have to acknowledge our agenda to be heard in a conversation and then quiet it; that agenda isn't more important than being present for the other person, especially if that person is someone you really care about. Your priority is to learn, not share.

4. Ask More Questions

Not only are we not going to chime in on the person we're listening to with our own two pennies, when we do have the chance to speak, we're going to ask questions to further clarify, understand, and learn from the person. Be mindful of how much you talk when the priority is to listen, so use your turns to speak to create more chances to hear from the other person.

5. Paraphrase

Paraphrasing means to express what someone else is trying to say using different words to gain more clarity. If you want to be sure you understood someone, say back to them what they just said to you. Don't be a parrot and repeat their wording, use your own words to communicate that you understand them. Paraphrasing will also ensure you don't misunderstand the person and end up responding to things they didn't even mean to say. Make sure you understand them before you say anything else in the conversation. A good prompt for this is saying, "So, what I'm hearing is . . . ," and share what they just said to you.

6. Acknowledge Fear

I used to hold people's words against them to a tee. I would make them feel bad if they weren't straightforward enough with me and required me to read between the lines. What I wasn't realizing is, not only did I need to read between the lines in what they were saying, I needed to listen closer to see the subtle reasons why they were saying it the way they were saying it. People don't want to offend or bother others, so they choose their words accordingly. Although this makes for poor communication, it reveals a lot about how they feel about themselves and you.

Them: "Hey, are you sure you want to watch *The Matrix* again?"

Me: "Yeah, I love that movie, why? You don't want to watch it?"

Them: "No, I'll watch it if you want to watch it."

Me: "Just @##$#$% say you don't want to watch it if you don't want to watch it!"

If I was really listening, I could have said:

Me: "Hey, don't be afraid to tell me if you don't want to watch *The Matrix*. I want you to be able to tell me without being afraid it'll cause drama, let's be open with each other."

Them: "Okay, I don't want to watch *The Matrix*."

Me: "Get out."[*]

---

[*] I'm kidding!

7. Admit If It's Too Much

Listening is more important when the things being discussed are hard to listen to. Sometimes we're overwhelmed with information, or things are triggering too many responses. You're of no value to the person you're listening to if you can't soak in what they're saying, so respect them and yourself enough to let them know if it's too much.

This is something I struggle with a lot. And it leads me to being a fixer and problem solver.

8. Listen to Learn, Not Fix

When someone comes to me with complaints and pain, I immediately want to help, and by help, I've realized I really just want to solve their problem so they will shut up. This is probably the origins of my first book, *Unlearn*. I wrote it because I was sick of hearing myself complain, so I wrote down very straightforward, blunt replies to all the things that hurt me. This is great for someone to read in the comfort of their own misery and home, but in person, trying to fix things may end up causing more damage. The reason we want to fix others' pain is because someone else's pain can activate our own pain and discomfort, which freaks us out. We don't know how to sit with pain,[*] so as the crazy creatures that we are, we respond by trying to numb, fix, and distract, all under the facade of helping. We have to realize we're not helping the other person; we're hurting them.

Sometimes it's because we don't have the answers, so we end up saying some corny cliché like, "Oh, everything happens for a reason" or "I'm sorry to hear that."[**] Instead, let's be okay with not having a perfect response. The

---

[*]   That's a whole other chapter.
[**]   Think about how you just made it about you when you said that.

goal isn't to respond, it's to listen. We are helping by being present. **The less energy we devote to fixing their problem, the more energy we'll have to listen to it, which in itself has healing qualities.**

9. Actually Wait Until They're Done Before Responding

Yes, I saved the hardest for last. Yes, you will have great counterarguments, points, personal anecdotes, etc., but none of those matter when the priority is listening. Once the other person is actually done, then ask if you can share a relevant moment or story. Don't go overboard—let's keep the focus on them— and make sure anything you say has no other agenda beyond being of value to the other person.

If we want to create more pathways to love in our life, we're going to have to do the work to become more active, generous listeners for others and our- selves. It's not easy, and you won't ever perfect it, but there's value in getting better. I've been practicing these tips myself, and it does get exhausting, but it's still better than the broken connections I'd been living with up to this point.

We feel lonely when we're not heard, and often the first step to being heard is to be the one listening. It's romantic to think that love is easy, when really it's realized through practicing skills we think should come naturally. Being quiet and listening, as uneventful as it sounds, will do wonders to further widen and open new pathways of love in our lives, and if love is the goal, this is a wonder- ful set of steps in the right direction.

TO LOVE IS TO UNDERSTAND.
TO UNDERSTAND IS TO LISTEN.

53.
LOVE IS ATTUNEMENT

I remember being a child, waking up in the middle of the night with the sudden urge to throw up. I ran to my door and began vomiting. I couldn't turn the door handle because it was covered in vomit. Once I finally got it open, I dashed to the bathroom and threw up in the sink and began crying.

My mom, who had to be up in the morning for work, woke up and surveyed what had just happened. She began to get upset, and the first thing she said to me was, "Why did you throw up in the sink instead of the toilet?" Even at that young age, I knew that wasn't the response I wanted. I was sick and scared and I needed my mom, but instead I got yelled at about the mess I made and the noise I caused.

That's a subtle example of the type of traumatic experiences that carry on into adulthood. Those moments when we feel like we don't matter. When our feelings are continually discounted, ignored, or reprimanded, then we're not shown how to respond to, express, or soothe our feelings as we get older. I've seen this manifest in myself as an adult, where I struggle to empathize with people who show weakness. I developed a "suck it up" attitude as a way to defend myself from letting anyone else down ever again. That's what trauma does, it teaches us how to work around the shortcomings of others, thus creating more shortcomings in ourselves.

I would catch myself being short with others who complain a lot. If I didn't get compassion and empathy, then those things wouldn't be afforded to others, even those who meant the most to me.

These old coping mechanisms create barriers to the flow of love in and around our lives, so something's gotta give.

That something is attunement.

Attunement goes beyond walking in someone's shoes. Instead, it's entering into their skin. It goes beyond empathy because it focuses on a two-way connectedness that prioritizes reciprocity and responses that actually resonate. To put it simply, attunement is being a mirror to the other person and yourself, really feeling what they feel, and responding in a way that truly matters. Our ability to be attuned comes down to how connected we are to others in the moment, and how clearly and effectively we can communicate that to them.

Attunement is the reactiveness we have to another person. It is the process by which we form relationships. Attunement comes across as genuinely caring for a person. Dr. Dan Siegel, a clinical professor of psychiatry at the UCLA School of Medicine, says, "When we attune with others we allow our own internal state to shift, to come to resonate with the inner world of another. It's making it as clear as possible to someone that their experience matters."

Before you take the sharp corner of this book and attack all those who never showed you attunement growing up, realize it's a fairly new concept that most people don't have on their tool belt. Attunement is something mostly practiced by therapists and other wellness professionals, so I can't hold it against my mother for not having it preprogrammed. But recognizing this and adding it to our tool belts is a chance we have to not only better our relationships with others, but to improve our relationship with ourselves and move beyond certain traumas of our past. All of this will deepen our experiences with love.

Here are three key ideas to remember around practicing attunement:

1. Start Recognizing, Labeling, and Accepting Your Own Emotions

Attunement starts at home; we have to be able to recognize our own emotions before we can recognize the emotions of others. When we make it a priority to be aware of our emotions, we can also start questioning them. Am I upset, or just hungry? Am I mad at them, or just feeling unheard? When we examine our emotions, we play the blame game far less.

2. Shift Your Focus to Understanding What the Other Person Feels

It's a golden rule we learn in elementary school: seek to understand before seeking to be understood. We often look at someone else's behavior in terms of what it means to us, but we have to flip that script. The way we question our own emotions, let's question theirs, try to be in their skin and meet them where they are, without making it about us.

3. When Talking to the Other Person, Try to Identify the Emotions They Are Feeling

This means asking questions to understand instead of placing judgment. Something as simple as, "I can understand why that would make you feel upset" or "I'm sorry you had to experience that" goes a long way to creating a genuine connection.

This is easier said than done, because oftentimes our first reaction is to be defensive. But we have to move beyond *reacting* and focus on *responding*.

This means making an active effort not to invalidate someone else's feelings, even if blame is placed on you. We get defensive when we make it about us first, and by doing so we can easily make it worse.

Attunement isn't a fancy word for empathy; empathy is a part of attunement. Attunement is getting down to a child's eye level and connecting with them after they've just thrown up and are feeling sick and scared. It's reassuring them that they'll feel okay. It's not telling your partner that you know how they feel, it's SHOWING them. It's actively listening, being open that there's more than one way to look at things, and prioritizing understanding over judgment.

Attunement is getting on the same page to create harmony between you and the other person, because when that happens, love flows between you in abundance. This applies to romantic partners, friends, people we work with, and family.

Now back to my mother.

In no way am I saying my mother is a bad person because of how she reacted. She grew up in a different time with different tools, and who among us is at our best after just being woken up in the middle of the night? In fact, with my sisters' kids, my mother has gone the other way, being extremely accommodating and empathetic, even when they're acting like brats.[*] She's a grandmother now who doesn't have to wake up early for work, and she can dedicate her time to being more present for her family.

Practicing attunement includes having compassion and making an effort to understand those who didn't know how to make us feel safe and secure all the time. To assume our parents would have known how to attune to us automatically is like expecting Shakespeare to know how to set up a wireless printer.

---

[*]   Love you Big Head, Eena, Zoe, and Nibz!

ATTUNEMENT GOES
BEYOND WALKING
IN SOMEONE'S
SHOES. INSTEAD,
IT'S ENTERING INTO
THEIR SKIN.

54.

CONFLICT STYLES

I have a sharp tongue. I put words together well and when I'm upset I tend to use those powers in very unhealthy ways. If I don't feel heard, I double down, and instead of using effective communication to get an idea across, I become a sniper, figuring out the right combination of words to get under the other person's ribs.

I don't want to be like that when I'm upset, and I immediately regret it when I see the change in the other person's eyes. It feels good to get things off our chest, but we can overdo it and cause damage beyond the issue at hand. There are different ways to handle conflict well, but before we can explore those, we have to explore the different ways we don't handle conflict well. If we want to keep the flow of love open between us and those we care about, we have to prioritize how to keep the lines of communication open when we disagree on things.

Here are four ways we handle conflict in our relationships that cause more damage than good, blocking the flow of love between us:

1. Silence

We've all given and received the silent treatment at one point or another in our disagreements with someone we love. Sometimes things get so overwhelming, we decide to shut down completely, tune out, turn away, act busy, or just distract ourselves with something else. There's no longer acknowledgment of the problem, or any communication to find a solution.

I get it, we don't always immediately turn silent, sometimes we try to communicate our side of things, and when it doesn't work, we decide being quiet is better than saying anything else. Sometimes we feel so attacked and overwhelmed, we just shut down. Sometimes we're triggered by things the other person says and we couldn't get a word out if we tried.

As understandable as it is to have this reaction, it doesn't make things better. This puts up a big stone wall between you and the person you care about and blocks both communication and love. It can be frustrating to the other person and make them feel like they don't matter.

Instead, if you feel overwhelmed in a disagreement, ask to take a break from the conversation, but *promise to return* to it after some time. Take 30 minutes to do something else, like taking a walk, writing in your journal, doing some active breathing.[*] And then return to the conversation from a place where you're more likely to respond rather than react. "Let's revisit this in 30 minutes/tomorrow morning" is better than shutting down completely and walking out the door without any explanation. The goal is to reduce anxiety, not feed it.

2. Defensiveness

In disagreements, we can often feel attacked, and sometimes we're right. We get defensive to thwart those attacks, as they can be overwhelming, especially when we feel those attacks are unjust. Getting defensive can mean we make excuses and play victim just to weather the storm and get the other person to back off.

---

[*]   Or building a voodoo doll . . .

Those excuses may have the opposite effect, however, of making the other person feel like we don't care. The more we defend, the more we may start to go on the offensive and start slinging blame and attacks. This only creates a cycle of finger-pointing and resentment, and further reduces the flow of love between us. **It's less about who's right or wrong, and more about bringing the stress down in the conflict.** Being defensive raises the anxiety of the disagreement, and taking some of the responsibility or making an effort to articulate the other person's perspective will do a lot to bring the tension down.

3. Criticism

A big mistake we often make when disagreeing is straying off the original topic and going at the other person. Out of frustration we can attack them instead of the issue at hand. This includes saying things to get under their skin, criticizing their character, using *always* and *never* statements, and making the issue bigger than it originally was.

We've all done this, and it's damaging. We can lie to ourselves and say it's constructive feedback, but it's really not. Recognize the difference between a complaint and criticism. Focus more on sharing how something makes you feel instead of telling the other person why you think they're wrong. This means using *I* statements more than *you* statements. And recognize that things will escalate quickly when we tear other people down.

Criticisms lead to resentment and contempt, some of the darkest emotions we have. Practice separating the person from their behavior. Let them know you care about them, but this one thing makes you feel shitty, and don't let the complaint snowball into other things. Instead of, "You never reply to my messages," try, "I feel like you don't care about me when my messages are ignored."

4. Meanness

Ever notice when you argue with someone and you impersonate them, it's always in a dumb mocking voice? Sometimes we're just outright dicks to each other, mocking, disrespecting, name-calling, being sarcastic, cutting them off—anything to make the other person feel they don't matter to us.

Whereas being critical is about what you say, being mean is in how you say it. Pay attention to your tone and tact.

This is probably us at our most primal, and we think brute force will make them see things our way. It's bullying in effect and causes a lot of damage beyond the disagreement. This level of contempt has an impact on our health and overall well-being. It is usually amplified by the power dynamic and is abusive by definition.

In romantic relationships, this is one of the largest indicators for divorce.

Maybe you grew up in a house that did this, maybe showing your fangs was a survival tool you needed growing up. I can understand that, but now you'll have to address this pattern of behavior from your past if you want a better future. Being mean may help you win the battle, but it will ensure you lose the war. There's little room for love when we decide being a jerk is an effective way to disagree.

Of course I'm guilty of this, and I've been working to do better. None of us came out of the womb knowing how to communicate, and few of us had healthy communication role models growing up. But none of that means it's okay to keep doing this.

If we want to experience more love in our life, we're going to have to do the work to become more effective communicators, and disagreements are the perfect places to practice.* Just being aware of these four bad habits will do wonders to get you responding more and reacting less, which will ensure things don't get worse than they need to be.

Psst... To read the bonus chapter HOW TO COMPROMISE to get actionable advice on finding areas where you need to set a boundary and where you can be flexible, scan this QR code:

---

*   Yes, it will take regular practice; reading a book doesn't shift behavior, it can only guide the work.

IF WE WANT TO EXPERIENCE
MORE LOVE IN OUR LIFE,
WE'RE GOING TO HAVE TO DO
THE WORK TO BECOME MORE
EFFECTIVE COMMUNICATORS,
AND DISAGREEMENTS ARE
THE PERFECT PLACES
TO PRACTICE.

55.
LOVE IS A GAME, AND GAMES SHOULD BE FUN

"My wife purposely let the garbage overflow as a sign for me to take it out."

"Did you take it out?"

"Hell no! I tied it up in a bag and put it in front of her shoes, that'll show her."

So many of our relationships feel like games, but with the wrong objective. Instead of enjoying the game or building a stronger connection from it, we devote our energy to trying to win, through seeking power. Power dynamics are real in relationships and can't be ignored. But, **if we choose power over connection in our relationships, we won't be left with much of either.**

Love isn't a prize we win, it's the game we keep playing; so let's ensure fun is the priority. Let's stop making it about winning and instead work to ensure everyone involved wants to continue playing. In play, and in life in general, forcing people to do things our way rarely works, and eventually someone is going to go home, taking their ball with them.

Having a strategic approach to love takes away the decency of the experience. Trying to manipulate every interaction to get a leg up on the other person may give you some temporary power, but in the long run it will leave you exhausted, unfulfilled, and further away from love. Instead, let's play in a way that keeps those around us enthusiastic to keep playing too.

All the passive-aggressive tactics we've inherited from the adults in our lives don't serve us well when trying to build a real connection. Connections don't need to be forced, they're developed the longer we play together. You can't make someone become your friend and you can't make someone fall in love with you, but you can create an environment that keeps them around, and the main ingredient in that environment is fun.

That means flirting more, complimenting more, and creating moments that feed anticipation, because everyone, without exception, enjoys having something to look forward to. Be silly, goofy, and informal. Change up the environment to create new memories and emotional responses with the people you care about, instead of being in the same old places that run the risk of triggering old undesirable feelings. Make a bucket list with your partner or friend and go through it slowly over a lifetime.

And for the love of everything, put the fucking phone away. Contrary to popular belief, phones DO NOT help make connections, it's the opposite. This world of constant distractions makes deciding where you place your attention a big priority. Let someone know they matter by putting that attention on them.

"Decency is the absence of strategy."
— Chögyam Trungpa

Our need for control has us playing dangerous games with people we love; this isn't sustainable, and it leaves us empty and uninspired to grow the relationships. The game of love, as complex and gut-wrenching as it can feel sometimes, has to be fun. We have to prioritize keeping the game alive much more than trying to win. This is a marathon, not a sprint.

None of this discounts the challenges that come from coexisting with someone for a long time. We can't make everything fun, and the most important parts of our lives, the maintenance functions, are often repetitive, routine, and unsexy. Seeing a pile of trash on your shoes after a long day of work isn't going to put butterflies in your stomach, but we can't romanticize a smelly kitchen either. I do notice when everyone is having fun, the necessary boring things can still get done. It's like having a puppy who wants to play all day—they keep it fun, but at the same time, there's necessary training and responsibilities around them that also need to happen.

In games, you can't win or lose when the goal is to have fun, so turn off the Amy Winehouse for a moment and throw on the Cyndi Lauper instead.[*]

---

[*]   Am I dating myself with these references?

LOVE ISN'T A PRIZE WE WIN, IT'S THE GAME WE KEEP PLAYING.

56.

IS HONESTY A PATHWAY TO LOVE?

Inspired by my friend Aubrey Marcus, I began practicing radical honesty in hopes that it would open more flow of love in my life. It made sense on paper—the less you lie, the fewer lies you have to hold, the more self-respect you gain, the more love can flow within and around you.

Radical honesty is complete honesty on all fronts—share it, be it, live it, and express it in every way possible. I began this journey a few months ago to lighten my load in life and try to exist on a level of freedom I've never felt before. Did I attain a higher sense of self-worth? Did I connect with others and myself on a deeper level? Did living and expressing my unconditional truth brighten the colors and smells of existence? Well, it's complicated.

My first major truth bomb came in the form of realizing that I am dramatically more sensitive than I would ever admit.[*] For the longest time, I limited my definition of the word "sensitivity." I decided that since I didn't react to Internet haters and racist encounters, the word didn't apply to me. What I learned was that for me sensitivity wasn't simply if others could get under my skin, but also that I was sensitive to their presence and energy. Accepting this truth meant

_____

[*]   #cancerproblems

that I had to shed my outdated alpha-male survival armor, the same armor that kept me afloat during challenging times growing up. It meant admitting that I was vulnerable and not completely capable of handling everything that comes my way. I grew up thinking vulnerability was weakness, so this realization felt harsh and was a truth I didn't want to face. The beauty of accepting this truth, however, was that it empowered me to make more decisions to feel better, mainly through being mindful of with whom and where I was spending my energy and accepting that it would eventually chip away at me.

This truth helped me realize how I could better serve, and thus love, myself. It didn't feel good initially to accept this truth, but from it, growth, empowerment, and change for the better came; for me that meant more love in my life, and much less tension.

Now, when it came to those around me, radical honesty didn't always fare as well. I told a friend that I'd rather not have them over to watch the next Raptors playoff game because they're not really interested in the game and I only want to watch with my fellow hardcore fans. We were *Game of Thrones* geeks as well and had a similar policy when we held viewing parties for the final season. Although I shared my thoughts and feelings with as much love and respect as possible, I haven't heard from them again. I'm still unsure of how I could have addressed it better while still being completely honest, but keeping it real doesn't seem to have gone over too well.

I've had a few more situations where being completely honest with others yielded a negative reaction from them. Again, to the best of my abilities, I practiced being respectful and showing tact, but if you're not saying what people want to hear, they may not appreciate anything else. .

The pattern I notice with the truth is that no matter how much it's cushioned, it will still sting, and that people can only accept your words from where they're at. As I chase the truth to reveal the love within, I've had to prime myself to accept more truths, especially the inconvenient ones.[*] That's made me appreciate honesty, even when it's not in my favor. If others aren't on that journey, then results may vary.

Honesty clears the mind, and the clearer the mind, the more room there is for love to flow. It also filters out those who would prefer the pretty lies over an ugly truth; that allows honesty to serve as a quality control for the people you have in your life. This in turn also creates more room for those who accept you for your honest self, which will only amplify the love that flows in and around you.

When we have to deny our truth, bite our tongue, or overly censor ourselves for others, we can run the risk of feeling resentment. Being anything but ourselves isn't sustainable in the long term, and if we wear enough masks for long enough, we'll lose who we are and won't appreciate what we've become. All those feelings are going to reduce the love we feel for ourselves and others. None of us are perfect, but we have a gut that's worth trusting. That gut, or our conscience, is learning itself, but it's still one of the best friends we have. **Our relationship with ourselves is the most important one we have and sets the tone for any other relationship we'll enter.**

We'd be wise to not trap ourselves in relationships that don't align with our truths; that ends up being an expensive life decision that we'll be paying for in many ways. I get it, it's natural to want people to accept us, but if we have to be something else to achieve that acceptance, then it won't last very long. Instead, and as scary as it sounds, we have to seek out and find people that align with our authentic self. That means replacing the question *Do they like me?* with *Do they align with who I am?* We've always been taught to put our best foot forward and make a great first impression, but that can't be at the expense of who we truly are.

---

[*]   Doesn't it seem like most truths are super inconvenient?

Now, once we're in a relationship, should we be completely and radically honest? Although I'm a strong believer that our truths are more important than our relationship, I'm not sure being an open book is also the solution. Our relationship with ourselves dictates that we should have our own secret garden and safe spaces, and that should require boundaries from even our most intimate partners. Cultivating ongoing and ever-growing honesty with each other is great, but that radical honesty can still get us in trouble when it comes to the everyday.

If she asks me if I think her sister is pretty, I still have to figure out what she's really asking before answering YES.[*]

I do think holding a bit of burden around the truth with the people we care about the most is a worthwhile struggle. Our words mean much more to them than others' words. This also acknowledges that we can only express our truth as much as we understand it, so when the stakes are higher, STFU.

We should spend much more time learning, discovering, and articulating our truth as much as possible. Make it radical and uncompromised when it's worth sharing, but for me, the jury is still out about whether it should always be shared in every situation. Maybe it's my fear talking, but a quality lie to make the person you care about the most feel good about themselves is part of the vocabulary of a beautiful love language. **Speaking our truth is loving ourselves, and holding on to that truth can, in some cases, be loving others.**

---

[*]   I've said too much.

OUR RELATIONSHIP
WITH OURSELVES IS
THE MOST IMPORTANT
ONE WE HAVE AND SETS
THE TONE FOR ANY
OTHER RELATIONSHIP
WE'LL ENTER.

57.
WALLS AND WINDOWS

When it comes to our relationships, we build them with walls and windows. Where we place those walls and windows matters. This concept came from Shirley Glass,[*] a researcher who explored the idea of infidelity in relationships. People cheat for a variety of reasons, and if we simplify them, it has to do with needs not being met within that relationship. Now, those needs may not be met because they may not have been communicated, and that causes the structure of the relationship to form in an unhealthy way.

If you're with someone, you give them a window into you[**] and develop walls around both of you to block the rest of the world. When needs aren't met and communication isn't happening, things go into reverse. A wall is formed between you and your partner, and now there are windows surrounding you for everyone else to get a better view inside. We may create those windows for everyone else to meet needs that aren't being met within the relationship. We all know, and have been, that person that shares too much about the inner workings of their relationship with someone else, that strengthens the walls and windows in the wrong places.

---

[*]   How punny!
[**]   This window represents access to you, not ownership, but that'll be another chapter . . .

Boundaries around the relationship are just as important as boundaries within it. It's those outside boundaries that can get messy when needs aren't met and the relationship is in trouble.

I'm talking about NEEDS here, not wants; core needs are rarely negotiable, and maybe we don't even get to decide them. If we decide to have a partner, we should make an effort to express our needs as clearly as possible so our partner has an opportunity to try to meet them. I understand it's scary, and even sometimes embarrassing to share your needs with others; we risk being judged, rejected, and made to feel ashamed of who we are and what we require. As scary as it is to share our needs, it's much more terrifying not to do it and to have those needs unmet. Then, you turn to something or someONE else.

That's the window, the free, open, and honest sharing of feelings and ideas, and if you're in a partnership, between you is where the window should be built. It's not an open window, because we need boundaries, but it's a clean window so your partner can see through as clearly as possible.

This isn't to say that this should be the only window to your life. We have other meaningful relationships, ones that matter, and each of those important people should also have some access to you and free, clear space to be open and honest with their feelings as well. But if you want your relationship to be a priority, that's the window that should be the biggest.

Problems arise when people outside the relationship know more about parts of your relationship than the other person in it. That means the windows and walls are in the wrong places. If this disconnect continues, eventually there's a bigger wall between partners, and bigger windows between people outside the relationship. This is how affairs develop—the window between you and someone else is bigger and clearer than the one you have with your partner.

Cheating isn't always physical; late-night conversations and sharing moments of intense vulnerability can definitely make another person feel betrayed.

We have to work to recognize these subtle shifts in construction, and always to notice our part in where the windows and walls are. It's not just our partner's job to meet our needs, it's our job to know our needs and communicate them to our partner and have open conversations about what needs to happen for them to be met.

If we find it easier to be open and honest with others about our relationships, it's a sign that work needs to be done. The amount of work we do is dependent on how much we care to keep the relationship healthy and growing. Honoring our personal boundaries and the boundaries of our relationship are essential to ensuring that health and growth are steady.

If you create a window for someone else, don't be surprised if that results in a bigger wall between you and your partner. I've been guilty of this; sometimes it feels as if it just happens naturally. It doesn't; we either feed it or don't fight it, and either way we have to take some ownership for it.

Ask yourself, *Where are your windows? Where are your walls?* and you'll realize what's really important in your life.

BOUNDARIES AROUND THE RELATIONSHIP ARE JUST AS IMPORTANT AS BOUNDARIES WITHIN IT.

58.

JEALOUSY IS NOT THE RIGHT SIGN OF LOVE YOU'RE LOOKING FOR

I thought it was cute when someone I was seeing got jealous. Maybe they brought up a comment someone left under my photo or aggressively asked, "Which friend!?" when I told them I was going out with a buddy. It made me feel like I mattered. If they didn't get jealous, then they must not care enough about me. There's a romance to the possessiveness, but it's a pretty flimsy facade when you really think about it. We can't control other people, and our jealousy is a mechanism of control. The need for control is fear, and fear shrinks pathways to love.

This doesn't pertain just to romantic relationships. Jealousy exist within family relationships, friendships, business arrangements, and even neighbors. If the goal is to feel and share more love, then we have to address jealousy at its roots and abandon the idea that it's a healthy expression of love. Jealousy is a dialect of fear, and anytime we recognize fear, we have to face it to make room for love.

To start, there's a notable difference between jealousy and envy.

Envy = loving what somebody else has

Jealousy = fearing something you have will be taken away by someone else

Envy is seeing a happy couple and wishing you also had that in your life. Jealousy is seeing someone else talk to your partner and being afraid that your partner may get snatched away from you.

Envy can promote inspiration or resentment depending on the person. I've been envious of my friends and the things they've accomplished. Sometimes I see it as something motivating. Their success is proof things can happen, and if I apply myself I can get those same results. It gives me focus and drive, and clarity on how to get there. Other times, it makes me roll up into a ball of insecurity and say mean things to myself in my head. I tell myself they don't deserve what they have, and it should have been me instead. These thoughts aren't very beneficial to anyone, and I try to catch myself as soon as possible. As toxic as those thoughts are, they're normal and we shouldn't beat ourselves up for having them; instead, just be aware of them, observe what they reveal about you, and allow them room to pass.

I've admitted to Lilly that I was jealous of her on different occasions. Once was when she was a voice on *The Simpsons*, or when she got to hang out with President Barack Obama. What I should have said was I was envious. Many of us often conflate envy and jealousy. I wasn't afraid of losing anything. I just liked what she had.

I've been jealous of friends. Sometimes the only thing I'm afraid of them taking from me is attention. Sometimes they do, intentionally or not. It's not that the fears are unfounded, it's that they chip away at the love

I have for them, and for myself. Love won't automatically be the antidote to jealousy. We can love someone and still be both jealous and envious of them. What love can do is motivate us to work toward heading in the other direction. Depending on the circumstances, that opposite direction of jealousy can be called mudita.

Mudita is a Sanskrit word* meaning "pure joy unadulterated by self-interest." Simply put, it's being authentically happy when other people are happy, even if it doesn't benefit you. It's the literal opposite of jealousy.

Imagine being completely happy for someone else when they're happy, no envy, no jealousy, just a sheer unfiltered share of joy for them.

That means being authentically happy for a co-worker who gets a raise over you, not just smiling for the cameras like a runner-up in a beauty pageant.

That means being authentically happy for a sibling or family member who receives more praise and attention from others than you.

It also means finding joy if your significant other develops a special bond with someone else. This form of mudita has been coined *compersion*.

Compersion is feeling joy in seeing your partner have a romantic relationship with another.

No, compersion isn't a weird voyeuristic kink, it's another intense opposite of jealousy. Compersion is the recognition that we can't own other people. People can only let us in, and we should accept them letting us in graciously. Jealousy associated with monogamy is rarely associated with the other person; we're not thinking about them, we're thinking about ourselves.

---

* *Karma* and *yoga* are also Sanskrit words; if you can remember those, you can remember *mudita*.

Compersion may be a bit too intense for some, but it's a real idea, and those that practice it genuinely do it from a place of combating the love-blocker that is jealousy. Whether it's your cup of tea, or if you're good with just mudita for now, recognizing that we need to distance ourselves from feelings of jealousy is important if we want to be better at and to feel more love in our lives.

If you love someone, finding happiness in their happiness is a direction we should aim for. Jealousy can lead to resentment, and resentment can feed *schadenfreude*—that's a German word for finding joy in the unhappiness of others. In other words, jealousy will make you a hatin' ass hater. Schadenfreude hurts everyone involved, and further closes the paths for love to flow. Schadenfreude is one of the worst versions of ourselves we can be. Do whatever you can to avoid resentment, even if that means starting conflict; resentment is the lowest place we can be, and it does the most damage to our pathways of love.

It's okay to feel jealousy; just be aware of it and recognize its impact on the love you want to experience in your life.

I'VE BEEN JEALOUS OF FRIENDS. SOMETIMES THE ONLY THING I'M AFRAID OF THEM TAKING FROM ME IS ATTENTION.

59.

NICE GUYS DON'T FINISH LAST

I had the biggest crush on this girl, and someone let her know. Back then I thought she was completely out of my league and learned quickly that she really enjoyed the attention. We ended up hanging out, and then hooking up. I got worried that she'd think I was using her, while she was worried I was catching feelings. In the end I was honest with her and expressed that I liked her more than a casual hookup, after which she promptly stopped talking to me.[*]

I shared too many feelings, and that made me less fun and mysterious to be around. It made me a simp.[**] I kicked myself over the experience, realizing that staying quiet would have easily given me a fun summer with a girl I had a massive crush on. Instead, it was a short-lived fling, and now I had to avoid her at every social event.

Over the years, I changed my behavior to avoid being a simp again. I would play it cool, even if my emotions were getting the best of me on the inside. All my texts were carefully crafted, and every encounter with a girl was strategic and rehearsed so I wouldn't seem out of my element, too needy, or too much into her.

---

[*]   The kids call that *ghosting*.
[**]   *Simp* is a slang insult for guys who are seen as too attentive and submissive to women. Famous simps include Milhouse from *The Simpsons* and any other doormat guy you've come across.

I figured it'd be better to be cool than to be myself.

The challenge a lot of people face in love is that they don't have great role models to look up to. All the alphas I knew were caricatures more than real people: the rock star, the athlete, the player, the thug. There was no one in my life, or in the media, to model for me how communication and connection would lead to a more genuine relationship with others. I always assumed I had to be someone else, and that if any girl liked me after seeing me without my mask, well then something must be wrong with her. So I kept playing it cool and being easygoing, even in situations where cool and easygoing were the last things I wanted to be.

Every so often, the facade would implode, I'd lose my composure, have an outburst, and ruin everything. Other times, my easygoing-ness was taken advantage of and other people who played the guilt game would get prioritized over me. I would get canceled on the most and made less of a priority because I wouldn't make any drama about it. **This game was frustrating, until I realized I didn't have to play.**

Not everybody is going to punish you or take advantage of you for being vulnerable, and the ones that do are telling you more about their story than yours. These experiences made me closed off to others who were being vulnerable with me. I thought they were being weak when really I should have been making space for them, like I wished others made space for me.

Nice guys don't finish last, guys who aren't nice to themselves do.
We think we have to be something else to please others, but that's not sustainable. There are people that won't run when we take off our masks, and those are the same people that can also help us learn a lot about ourselves. I thought I needed to make up for the defeat of that crush by being successful with other girls, but none of that was going to address how low I was feeling on the inside.

I put myself out there and it bit me in the ass. But more important than the outcome was the fact that I put myself out there. **Staying true to ourselves is a bigger victory than what we accomplish being anyone else.** It took me years to realize that it's okay to feel things and admit them to other people, even at the risk of scaring them away. The alternative is always adapting and adjusting to what we think others want from us, only to end up exhausted or to forget who we really are.

This doesn't just apply to relationships with people. I experienced this with my art and career, thinking I wasn't allowed to share my truth because I might get rejected by the audience or the people who could open doors for me. What I didn't know at the time was **anything I got from not being myself really wasn't mine.** When we can be ourselves, we find more peace, and the more peace we find, the less external distractions and medication we chase to make things feel better.

So let's all further the art of being ourselves. If someone thinks that makes us weak, that's their problem, not ours. I had my simp phase and I'm proud of it, it was more true to myself than any alpha-male facade I could ever present. **Let's not lose ourselves trying to keep others around—that's an expensive decision to make.**

NICE GUYS DON'T FINISH LAST, GUYS WHO AREN'T NICE TO THEMSELVES DO.

60.
WHEN TO CLOSE PATHWAYS OF LOVE (WHEN TO END RELATIONSHIPS)

Let's keep it simple: we can talk about all the things that make our relationships good and bad, but the most important thing is how that relationship makes you feel about yourself. It doesn't matter what type of relationship it is, we can be talking about friendships, family, or your imaginary relationship with the cute guy who delivers your pizza.[*]

Our relationships show us where we have abundance and lack.

The people in our lives open pathways to love for us, but that's not always the case with every person in our lives. Every so often when things start to feel bad enough, we start to think about letting go. The first chapter in this book is me sharing when I had to do this with someone I cared about deeply, and it was easily one of the most difficult decisions I had to make, and definitely one of the most challenging chapters of my existence. As hard as it was to endure, it was just as hard, if not more so, to even start having that conversation with myself.

---

[*]   There's a joke about extra dipping sauce here.

It's ironic to read about ending relationships in a book about experiencing more love, but it's an important part of the journey. Unfortunately not all relationships serve us the same, or give us opportunities to be of service to others. These relationships can then be the reason our pathways to love are shrunken or non-existent. We all know, or have been, that person who lost themselves trying to keep a relationship alive. That loss of self is an expensive outcome to keep other people around, and we have been willing to end a relationship for a greater good.

It's not always clear in a relationship what a red flag or a deal breaker is. A lot of that can depend on our own deep values, whether it's a friend or a business or romantic partner, we can always rely on the simplest question: "How do they make me feel about myself?"

My friend Eva said,[*] **"Good love makes us feel larger in a larger world, bad love makes us feel smaller in a smaller world."** We can't always put words to feelings, or even pay attention to how we feel around the people in our lives, but it's worth making it a priority and paying attention to it.

Here's a long, but not exhaustive, list of reasons why letting go of a relationship may be for the greater good. Again, this can apply to all relationships, not just romantic ones.

- We keep making excuses and hoping things will improve in a hypothetical future: "Once we live together/get engaged/finish school, things will get better."
- You feel the need to tone down yourself to protect others. You feel too afraid to ask the other person to take on and accept your reality.
- You feel pressure to change and not be your authentic self.
- You only feel their love and support when you're in a good place. You feel a pressure to maintain emotional stability, because when shit hits the fan, they can't be there for you. This makes you feel guilt, shame, and anxiety for being a human with highs and lows.

---

[*]   And I'm quoting her to avoid a lawsuit or wedgie.

- They're rarely willing to dive into your world or meet your friends and family, or they already have you anxious about even asking them to do so.
- You feel negativity and anxiety around them. You often feel like you're walking on eggshells. Everyone has their own definition of *often*, and I understand that everyone is human and will do and say the wrong things to make us feel shitty every now and then. But even with that, the people that care about us will show remorse, and this will be heavily outweighed by positive experiences.
- You're made to feel that what you need doesn't deserve to be shared and isn't warranted. You feel needy and unreasonable anytime you want to share.
- In a romantic relationship, you don't feel secure when you're not together. This is less about trusting them and more about your attachment style, and how they help you manage that.
- **You're made to feel hidden in their life.**
- You don't feel safe to be yourself around them.
- The connection is wearing away slowly with resentments that are adding up. These resentments can be anything from substance abuse, to financial issues, to them having other relationships that make you feel less wonderful about yourself.
- Misalignments about what really matters. You can be sleeping in the same bed but dreaming different dreams. This can cause a tug-of-war where everyone loses.
- You're surprised when people compliment how nice and considerate they are.
- You're not certain they'll be there for you if shit hits the fan in a real emergency. You don't feel like your emotional or physical wellness is a priority to them.
- They care about impressing strangers more than you.
- You're most likely the person they target to put down.
- You feel like you can't be the partner they deserve.
- You're bored.

Sometimes we can't express a reason or even put our finger on it, but we feel it. **You don't need a reason to end a relationship, you can just trust your gut, and if you have to go, you're free to go.** Oftentimes we can force ourselves or others to hang on past their expiration date, and the result is less love and more uneasiness for everyone. Bad breakups, as much as they suck, are still better than dragging someone out long term.

There isn't a part of me that's acting like this is easy, and I'm sorry if you found something on the list that hit under the ribs and shattered a vision of what you thought you had. Self-love is about accepting ourselves for who we are, and also protecting spaces for us to be that authentic self. It also means we advocate for ourselves to be in the healthiest spaces and relationships possible, and that's going to involve some hard decisions.

I've been broken up with, had to break up with, and every variation in between, and it all sucks. **To be rejected or to reject another person is a deep pain.** I won't dare lie and say that deep pain is something everyone recovers from. Recovering from the loss of someone who really matters takes a lot of time and active work, but the alternatives to not honoring ourselves can be much more expensive.

Pain pushes us until vision pulls us, but every so often we can fall into the pit of pain and get stuck. **The dangers of staying in a relationship well past its expiration date can lead us into unhealthy spaces, like resentment and loss of self.** Being spiteful and resentful in life is a giant dead end to connecting with others and will only close pathways to love. Losing our sense of authentic self is a death while breathing. There really isn't a greater good beyond maintaining our sense of self and enjoying our own existence. Let's not romanticize sticking it out in a situation that does more damage than good. Doing that doesn't make us martyrs, heroes, or "ride or die" types, we're just allowing these relationships to chip away at us until there's nothing left and we turn to other destructive choices to compensate.

Don't stick together for the kids, don't fear the wrath of the gossips or the complications of mutual friends. **We're not failures in our lives because a relationship has to end** —if anything, ending a relationship is a more challenging journey than starting one, and those willing to take it for their greater good deserve our admiration, respect, and support. Let's not lose ourselves trying to keep others around.

We can't avoid heartbreaks, nor can we avoid breaking the hearts of others. Sometimes we have to lose a limb to save a life, and as unpleasant as that is, we're still alive. Let's honor love by ensuring it's a priority in our lives, and exercise that by closing pathways that are doing more damage than harm. I'm not saying it's easy, but if this chapter is connected with what you've already been feeling, I can promise you in the long run, it'll be worth it.

Psst... To read the bonus chapter HOW TO BEST CLOSE A PATHWAY OF LOVE to get actionable advice on breaking up and moving on, scan this QR code:

"GOOD LOVE MAKES US FEEL LARGER IN A LARGER WORLD, BAD LOVE MAKES US FEEL SMALLER IN A SMALLER WORLD."

61.

A BROKEN HEART IS AN OPEN HEART

While the weather was warm, I joined a friend at an outdoor yoga class. The instructor Geeta was awesome, holding free outdoor classes because she loved yoga and wanted to share that with others.

During the deepest stretches that we needed to hold for a long time, she distracted us with stories, and one story she told was about the young boy and his new heart.

There was a young boy in the village showing everyone his heart. It was clean, bright, and shiny, and he was really proud of how beautiful it was. A village elder noticed the boy showing off and said, "That's not a beautiful heart, this is a beautiful heart," and he proceeded to show his heart to all the villagers.* His heart wasn't clean, bright, or shiny, rather it was dull, worn, and scarred. The old man explained that a beautiful heart is one that's been worn and used. Doing things to preserve the heart from damage is the opposite of what it takes for that heart to be beautiful.

We make so many decisions in our lives to avoid damaging our hearts. We treat our hearts the way our grandparents treat furniture: it's

---

*   I'm assuming this is a magical village where people could just pull out their hearts without dying.

there, wrapped in plastic and not really meant to be used, it's just meant to exist and take up space. Our hearts aren't a brand-new pair of white sneakers we need to tiptoe through life in to avoid getting scuffed; they're work boots, meant to be tested, weathered, and destroyed. A broken heart is an open heart, and all the things we go through in life that bang our hearts up help develop our character, our wisdom, and our overall essence. Every person who's broken my heart has been my teacher, showing me both what I want and what I don't want in the world of love. Every heart I've broken also revealed something I needed on my journey of love.

Heartbreaks suck, but they really are essential.[*] It teaches us lessons a life without damage would never reveal. We learn that life isn't predictable, and that at any moment, our entire understanding of comfort can be flipped on its head. Heartbreak teaches us that we can love and hate someone at the same time, and the apparent contradiction opens us to a world of compassion where there may not really be any good guys or bad guys. Heartbreaks force us to rely on ourselves for survival, and free us from the toxic idea that someone else is responsible for the smile on our face. It helps set our journey of self-improvement by putting a spotlight on our weaknesses. Heartbreaks show us how inconsistent and unreliable our emotions are. It sobers us up with the truth that love isn't enough to keep people together.

Most important, it reminds us of an obvious, but ignored truth: life goes on.

Sometimes the only memory we have of love from the past is the scar it left.

A broken heart opens and teaches us a lifetime's worth of lessons in the most painful ways, and as much as it sucks to feel, it's important to experience.

---

[*]   Waddup, *Unlearn* reference?

I'm writing this chapter still in the thick of my self-imposed heartbreak, and the wave of pain is overwhelming, but so revealing. **The heart never breaks the same way twice, so going through one doesn't always prepare you for the next.**

I may not be doing a great job of selling enthusiasm toward heartbreak, but I'm sure if it hasn't already, it will find you, and once it does, I hope some of my words connect and add clarity to your journey. The emotions and the pain are real, and they can manifest physically and do damage, but so many before us have felt and survived it; so can you.

I told myself that I've experienced enough heartbreak to never fear it again, but that's not true. I fear rejection, loss, and making mistakes just as much as I ever did, if not more. My choices subconsciously try to protect me from getting hurt, but that also sabotages me from building real connections. When I feel that fear, I try to sit in silence until I find that quiet voice in me that whispers to me at the height of the pain, *You'll grow through this, you always do.*

Opening our hearts further widens pathways of love we have for the people that are still in our lives, as well as for ourselves.

Let's take the plastic off and Rick James the couches of our hearts. Let's wear them in and find the magic in their cracks instead of building fortresses around them, rotting away their potential.

HEARTBREAK TEACHES US THAT WE CAN LOVE AND HATE SOMEONE AT THE SAME TIME.

YOU DON'T KNOW LOVE: A *love* STORY

Over the years, all of our adventures around the world involved us stumbling through a foreign place, lost, unable to make smart choices, trying to figure out how to get back to our hotel, or find a meal, or get some weed; it was always an adventure, with a side dish of surrender.

This was my fake fiancée from the staff Christmas party I mentioned earlier in the book. The one that was the first to say to me, "The world needs to hear Humble The Poet," and although the world began to hear from me, she ended our relationship and took off on her own adventures to South Korea, where she seemed less interested to hear from me. Over the next 10 years we'd cross paths in Bali, the United Kingdom, and Dubai, but here we are now, in the most touristy part of our hometown, Toronto, waiting for our nachos, sitting in the rain, watching others scramble for shelter.

"This is so beautiful, I love the rain, I love being here with you, I love this moment," she says.

"You've always been good at recognizing these moments," I say.

"Aren't you?"

"No, I only see them because you show me."

"Ahh, Kummer!" Only my family called me Kummer. It was a nickname based on my sisters' inability to pronounce *Kanwer* when we were kids. "You don't know nothing about love. You're writing a book about it, but you know nothing about love, Kummer." She didn't sound critical or condescending, she sounded sympathetic, as if I was color-blind and staring at a rainbow.

"You're right," I said, even though I didn't mean it. It was a rare occasion when my urge to debate was less important than enjoying the moment.

"Be selfish, have kids, then you'll know love. . . . Fuck! You'll know love then, Kummer, have kids. No, actually don't do it, because climate change is fucking up the planet, but if you can ignore that and be selfish, have kids, then you'll live life to the fullest, then you'll know love!"

I thought about my friend Amit talking about his first kid: "It's so much work, man, I don't get any sleep, and it's expensive, and your whole life is based around them, it's fucking hard . . . but shit, I want another one, or two, and I don't know why!"

It was a much less romanticized view of children compared to hers. He was being honest about the whole experience, and whatever biological switches were flipped as a result. I could have brought this story up, but instead I continued my passive resistance for the greater good.

"You're right."

"But don't do it, cause there's no turning back, but I'm telling you, Kummer, I don't love anything like I love my kids, they make you alive. People don't like having kids because they forgot what it means to be a kid. My kids let me be a kid, my kids see the real me, and just love me. I get to see the world through their eyes. It's so much more beautiful through their eyes."

In a world where experiencing love seems like so much work, it starts to feel like having kids is Mother Nature's way of making it all seem worth it. After all, we're keeping her happy by sticking to the script she imperfectly designed us for.

"You're right."

"But fuck, I have so much anxiety, I couldn't sleep last night thinking about all the floods and global warming. What are my kids going to do!? But maybe it doesn't matter, maybe just bringing them into the world is enough, and it doesn't matter if this whole world goes to shit. At this point it's a selfish decision, but if you really want to know love, if you really want to live life, have kids. Why are you even writing a book about love if you don't have kids?"

At this point, depending on whether you have kids or not, you have strong opinions on her views. And unlike me, you aren't living a moment in the rain from *The Notebook* to let it slide. I didn't feel like she was being a gatekeeper deciding on whether I experienced love. Rather, I felt like she wanted me to feel what she felt, maybe in hopes that I could put it in better words and recruit more people to have ugly, smelly children.

"I'm gonna use this story in my book and not give you credit."

She laughs.

"Fuck, I love this so much. I love being with you. Ahh, this weather is so shitty, we're soaked."

"Let's go get our nachos."

"Okay."

As we eat the nachos back at my place, my puppy, Boogie, gives me the eyes. I look down and wave my hands from side to side, signaling that I have no food left. It's my attempt to teach her that she won't be getting any table scraps tonight.

Seconds later, I throw a couple nachos her way and she begins to feast.

"You're going to make such a great father," she says laughing at my defeat. "You already are."

62.
THE LAST BOOK I'LL EVER WRITE

I'm writing this four hours after the deadline to submit this manuscript to my publishers.

The first Guru of Sikh philosophy, Sri Guru Nanak Dev Ji, wrote: "If you want to play the game of love, then step onto the path with your head on the palm of your hand."

It's been 20 months since the breakup that I spoke about in the intro to the book. Sometimes I say the breakup inspired the book, but really it was the book that inspired the breakup.

The theme of this book, and every other book I write, is to let go to gain more, and as I began the journey of trying to understand and experience love, it required me to let go of one of the most important and beautiful relationships I ever experienced.

Sacrifice is a dialect of love.

Today, 20 months after that breakup, I'm happy to announce I've since met my nex . . . my new soulmate, and we're expecting our first child in the spring, and we just bought a farm in the country with chickens, horses, pigs, and a unicorn.[*]

---

[*]   Isn't it odd that it's not AN unicorn? English is a strange language.

Of course, I'm lying.

A year after the breakup, I was still chasing rebounds and screaming, "I can't believe I almost got married!" sometimes with the joy of a guy who dodged a bullet, but more often with a deep, miserable tone of regret. A few months later I moved from Toronto to Los Angeles, a voluntary step into the unknown, and a lot more discomfort than I could have ever imagined.

A month ago, my once-fiancée[*] was in town, and over a call to plan a hangout, she shared some of the most challenging moments she's endured and the most difficult choices she has made since the breakup. There was a lump in my throat the whole time, and the next day I called to cancel our plans to meet up. She agreed and shared that she also realized she wasn't ready to see me.

Two weeks ago, on a call with my mother, she casually said, "You would have been married for two years now."

I can't speak Punjabi well enough to effectively tell her how much that hurt to hear; I haven't spoken to her since.

The last few months have also included an increased amount of time, energy, and attention to all the things that shrink my pathways of love: choosing short-term gratification over long, unhealthy foods, women that I know I'm not compatible with, friends I don't connect with, and way too much social media.

Why am I telling you this?

Well, if you made it to the end of the book, I owe you this level of truth. I, like you, have my good days, and not so good days. You see, **the struggle to experience love is much like having to choose between a plate of broccoli, and a box of French fries.** We all know which one we should choose, we don't need to read a whole book to figure that out, but even if we

---

[*]   Stings less than saying "my ex"

did read a whole book, or even write a whole book on the subject, that still doesn't mean we'll choose the green, steamy goodness over the delicious, greasy carbs.[*]

I ignored my own research and advice most of the time over the course of writing this book because, like the epic battle of broccoli vs. French fries, knowing better doesn't guarantee that we'll do better.

Reading a book can't make us automatically experience more love in our life, no matter the title, but one thing it can do is make us more aware.

I'm not living perfect days, but I am more aware of the impact of each decision. I can connect my choices to their consequences more clearly. That clarity allows me to explore more options to feel better, to allow more love in my life.

The clarity in this book can do the same for you.

I've since invested in a therapist, and a personal trainer, and my new puppy, Boogie, and I spend at least 90 minutes at the park every day. I'm no longer living in a world of duality—it's not the whole plate of broccoli vs. the whole box of fries. I can take pieces from both and notice the difference in how I feel depending on which I take more of.

Looking at life beyond duality opens a pathway to love, a life where things aren't *this* vs. *that*, but instead, *this*, *that*, and *everything in between*. I, like you, am not leaving this book a love guru, but instead, I'm leaving it with my struggles intact and injuries still fresh, but my eyes are open much wider. **Being hurt unexpectedly is trauma and can lead to cynicism. Being hurt and learning from it leads to open eyes, and that feeds courage.**

Let's use what we've learned to be courageous enough to experience more love.

---

[*] At this point I also feel the need to bring up poutine. If you're not Canadian and have no idea what that is, you're not living life.

Love is an action, and that action requires practice every day. Some days are easier than others and accepting that will take us a long way toward keeping those pathways open.

This may be the last book I ever write. It's not that there aren't other things to write about—it's just that what's required to get this book finished, and the even more laborious work required to make sure you know it exists, does little to promote pathways to love. I love myself enough to admit that my well-being is more important than some money and notoriety.

To experience love, we have to let go. In Sikhi, the metaphor for sacrifice is giving your head. I've been shedding an old life over the past few years to make space for love to flow, and I'm realizing I still have a ways to go.

Sacrifices don't feel like sacrifices when they're done for love. If you want to walk the path you've been reading about in this book, expect sacrifice, expect loss, and expect the death of your former self; it's not all *or* nothing, love allows it to be all *and* nothing.

I'm excited for you on your journey, and I'm terrified for me,[*] and if we never cross paths again, just know, from the bottom of all that fucking matters, I love you for making the time to read my words and wish for nothing but the most amazing transformations for you on your journey.

Remember to always choose love.

Be love, my beloved.

— Kanwer

---

[*]   Courage is feeling the fear and doing it anyway.

THE STRUGGLE TO
EXPERIENCE LOVE IS
LIKE HAVING TO CHOOSE
BETWEEN A PLATE OF
BROCCOLI AND A BOX OF
FRENCH FRIES.

ABOUT THE AUTHOR

Humble The Poet (aka Kanwer Singh) is a Canadian-born artist, rapper, spoken-word poet, international best-selling author, and former elementary school teacher. He is the author of *The Globe and Mail* bestseller *Unlearn* and *Things No One Else Can Teach Us*.

With his tattoos, beard, head wrap, and silly smile, Humble commands attention. He stimulates audiences with ideas that challenge conventional wisdom and go against the grain, with dynamic live sets that shake conventions and minds at the same time.

He has performed at concerts and festivals, including Lollapalooza, and has been featured in major media including *The New York Times*, *BuzzFeed*, *Vogue*, *Rolling Stone*, and *Huffington Post*.

Visit him at HumbleThePoet.com.

ACKNOWLEDGMENTS

Hundreds of you preordered the book before it had a cover to judge, and before any pages were printed to browse.

That means a lot, THANK YOU.

I'll continue to work my ass off to prove you right.

Madeline Lugo, Lynnette Kannangara, Lisa Walsh, Angel Wooster, Kayla Gabriel, Shana Roark, Kenny Griffin, Prabhnoor Singh, Paramveer Kahlon, Nicole Osborne, Maureen Fautley, Devion Boehnke, Adam Ross, Crystal Barnes, Meg Pendergrast, Natasha Gohil, Brittany Muller, Sophie Paige Howarth, Kendra Netzke, Michael David Velasquez, Dr. Tricia Rampersad, Ana Paret, Arlene Lawrence, Amen Kaur, Simon Carlsson, Artika Singh, Sumita Sikand, Montesha Gatlin, Andrew Bautista, Lynette Freeman, Raaghnie Autar, Sarah Haight, Bimal Ghundhu, Beth Hammann, Coley Brock, Allegra Pajot, Kiranjeet Gill, Navraj Grewal, Jillian Tarves, Sagar Trivedi, Ari Gaeta, Brittany Edwards, Sukhneet Sethi, Farha Shariff, Oscar Graciano, Harjeet Rathour, Rachel Lee, John Helm III, Celjan Rozko, Gurbir Mahl, Diana Sanchez, Lovejot Singh, Thresea Singh, Shandhra Ramana, Manmeet Singh, Esperansa Cervantes, Kami Singh, Sanantha Venkat, Akiba S, Preet Grewal-Hayer, Mamta Rana, Jasleen Uppal, Rebekah Markey, Robyn Lea, Jeanette Chin, James Liberato, Anish Chopra, Michael Wideman, Bhumi Patel, Simranjeet Kaur, Navjot Mehmi, Ana Paret, Jasneet Kaur, Toni Alberts, Mandy Schnurr, Navleen Naru, Davidorla Hunt, Paulina Singh, Amy Etrheim, Anne Belanger, Beats The Get Down Podcast, Jasmeet Singh Dhaliwal, Jordan Farmer, Sanjana Sankar, Lopes Monteiro Lina, Ricardo J. Alejandrez, Lee Nisbet, Pruthuvie C., Palvinder Singh Arya, Tejal Naik, Majtabah Walai, Adrian Gortych, Estela Chavez, Kamaljit Rai, Jacob Gregovich, Atenas Lozano,

Brendan Nahmias, Erinn Rodas, Deval Pradip, Preet Grewal Hayer, Nadja Katharina E. Kaplan, Jas Panesar, Vetosa Thompson, Dimitrios Mallinos, Alex Adler, Ryan Bednar, Connie Lozano Yoga, Karanveer Panesar, Sonam Chauhan, Graham Goddard, Vijay Mann, Amaneet Sanghera Khaira, Kimmy Williams, Camilla Persaud, Chanpreet Singh, Giovanni Gonzalez, Sebastian Gortych, Soyo Lane, Amber Medley, Komal Luthra, Sai Thanmae K, Mike Nowak, Chloe Impellizeri, Iain Fotheringham, Yeti Page, Deep Desai, Rokeia Stephens, Noor ul ain Kaur, Myron John Tataryn, Manmeet Arora, Myka Kandaké, AniSri JK, Leni Alexandria, Salma Mendoza, Yuki Sasaki, Lori Elaine Miller, Desa Davis, Barbara Lehtinieml, Ashley Winn, Oliver Bernat Lopez Yubero, Ron Romero, Dal Dosanjh, Theeran Sohal, Hardeep Mithra, Chuck Palalay, Pam Stortz, Hardik Shah, Prabhjot Shokar, Simranjeet Kaur, Monty Virdi Singh, Angel Huertas, Raheem Malik Kelsey, Anmol Singh, Liana Sudan, Kandis Robinson, Arshdeep & Rhythm Khabra, Frank Adams, Jaspreet Talwar, Sarah Flanigan, Izzy Grace, Giahna Glasco, Raman Jhalli, Juli Emmons, Alyia Chan, Luciano Contreras, Jonathan Edwards, Aidan Roth, Mayra Ramirez, Cara Lucio-Burge, Sukhjeet Kaur, Marly Dhaïti, Naseweis Hantschick, Manpreet Aulakh, Judith Matthias, Kundi Quest, Alex Gurchin, Nitik Kaushal, Anjna Singh, Saran Kanda, Vishal Solanki, Chloe Ladkin, Vishal Solanki, Dionne West, Christina Decker, Lauren Wirth, Jaclynn Villarreal, Krishna Morari, Anjulique "The Artist" Johnson, Sandy Kaur, Monica Kaur, Jennifer Sander, Sandy G, @B2FLSVG, Natsumi Yagi, Darnesia Cochran, Zahid Dossa, Kendall Saxon, Brian Hardy, Caroline Cheng, Patrick McNerney, Arminder Dhanki, Ayswar A, Braiden Ranstrom, Joshua Uhrig, Inayat Dhillon, Jenish Jeyakanthan, Ayesha Mehreen, Paris Bauldwin, Koumal Patel, Alieje Robinson, Antigone Cote, Sunny Johal, Amit Kapoor, Gaby Andrews, Johnny Della Luna, Michael Lin, Jaden Hohepa, Angelina Acevedo, Zack Spear, Minnie Dosanjh, Laura Gard, Esther Sanchez Zepeda, Monis Rose, Dimple Badhan, Rob Cooke, Vivian M Varela, Zoravar & Nirbaan Samra, Jayshri Dayal, Amar Kaur, Kurtis Wilde, Sakhsi Pushpinder, Robert McGarity, Gagan Bisla, Gaganpreet Kaur, Monica Rouse, Navjot Kaur, Surender Surender, Mehar Gandam, Amy Brewer, Jasdeep Shangari, Sat Sunny, Arun Murali, Virgen Diaz Vega, Shan Menton, Abdul Rehman Hassan, Mike Wideman, Kandis Robinson, Cazmir Leschke, Rupi Sidhu, Melissa Mae, Frances Hinojosa, Katie "Kid" Spry, Harvir Gill, Starr Sheppard-Decker, Cassandra Zubiate, Parm Bhullar, Christina Vasquez, Rami Mahal, Talya Hood Scott, Kevin Cleland, Jasmeen Dhinsa, Ravi Bhardwaj, Natalie Pellnat, Giselle Chan, Tania Carswell,

Jaisika Atwal, Aishah Abdullah, Jordan Antoine, Atchana Ganesalingam, Yeliz Sherifali, Sonia Sheth, Aysha Panatch, Melody Ricard, Rohit Kumar, Jen Raynak, Sanne Muijrers, Lisa Nolan, Roselena Arias, Sina Bacol, Harmanpreet Singh, Erica Morgan, Starra Kaur Sidhu, Sineha Maheshwari, Joanna Desormeaux, Rohit Kumar, Rania Yphantides, Amy Shereda, Marisha Mistry, Taranjit Singh, Steph Folger, Balj Bhangoo, Jag Atwal, Sangeeta Ramnanan, Vivienne Addams, Balbir Kaur Mokha, Rangat Singh, Saran Kanda, DeRhaun Mallett, Eva Giessauf, Kaamna and Saroj Dhindsa, Kiranjeet Gill, Rodrigo Marcuzzi, Raf Ullah, Narpal Singh Arya, Erin Hogan, Fantasia Willow Maraj, Chaz Whittington, Sukhjeet Kaur, Rachel Miele, Simon Carlsson, Sahi Arul, Alice Peck, Lisa Yannick, Sharon Mclaine Peguero Carreras, Kelsey Paige!, Munsimran Kaur Sekhon, Aakanksha Thakur, Suzy Darling, Demetrius Latham, Ph.D., Krishna Patel, Kiranjeet Gill, Alyssa Joy Lawenko, Cassie Zubiate, Rozelle Adora, Baljeet Singh Bharaj, Galileo Nkosi, Rajwant Katherine Singh, Arun Singh, Leva Kaleinikovaite, Joy Hammonds, Isuru Senaratne, Fat Bobby, Claire Stange, Amarpreet Ghataoura (my eucalyptus tree), Keanu Bailey, Fotiní Misthou, Didi Miller, Gurcharn Cheema, Milena Smodis, Tyecia Powell, Yusuf Atcha, Vyjayanthi Vadrevu, Ewelina Antoniewska, Jay Bathija, Carolyn Retana, Komal Randhawa, Tonia Nehil Enright, Bally Bainbridge, Justen Olmo, Stacy Bailey, Paul Mokha, Roshni Arora, Hanna Karlton, Péter Vargacz, Neha Kumar, Chris Holmes, Carmelle Gentle, Amarpreet Ghataoura, Ebony Lajoy Bell, Demetrius Latham, PhD, Toni Tallman, Megan Choi, Prabhjot Kaur, Ashley Forche, Lisa Almond, Jannette Carrazco, Tasha Cameron-wesley, Kristin Sims, Gunpreet Rekhi, Anish Chopra, Yeliz Sherifali, Hargun Hansrao, Veronica Becerra, Sherri Martin-Saggiomo, Harjot Kaur, Anaïs Lurion, Liberty Martin, Jeremy Markey, Yashasvine Dandothikar, Ash McMichael, Anni Low-A-Chee, Simran Saini, Marie Atrophy, Prem Khullar, Brittany Phillips, Travis Eubanks, Vashon Williams, Bobby Karmakar, Ja'Toya Taylor, Divya Kapoor, Amarjyot Narang, Jayneet Chhabra, Jaime Ramsey, Sabine Schueller, Jennifer McLean, Terence Douglas, Sunita Kaur, Sarbjit Raja, Sean Gorendar, Samantha Cruz, Ramir Milay, Lailee Khan, Gurdev & Balbir Mahl, Aarti Doshi, Sahaj Kohli, Kara Colynuck, Daniella Bissember, Karen Dhaliwal, Marie-Eve Carmichael, Pindi Rai, Aman Gill, Dann Benjamin, Nikah LeDet, Juhi Laungani, Tarundeep Shah Singh, Vikramjeet Singh, Kamaljit Rai, Tara Sebastian, Navneet Kaur, Sanjay Verma, Julianne Neal, Rachel Gough, Chirag Dhamija, Sathi Suprai, Michelle Cain, Andrew Bautista, Amrit Barn,

Monique Mazur, Lucy Gutierrez, Ola Subeh, Kristin Carlsson, Bhoomi Bhatt, Alisha Molina, Harishta Kaur, Madhura Kode, Cobb Keen, Brooke Janousek, Mandeep Kaur Nijjer, Ashley Miller, Meharpreet Singh, Shivanee Sujata, Simon Carlsson, Yousef Erakat, Nick Bassi, Erwin Mankoo, Trisha Lochan, and Sukhjeet Kaur.

. . . and to everyone else who preordered but didn't follow instructions to submit their name before the print deadline, a bushy bearded kiss has been blown in your direction.

We hope you enjoyed this Hay House book. If you'd like to receive our online catalog featuring additional information on Hay House books and products, or if you'd like to find out more about the Hay Foundation, please contact:

Hay House, Inc., P.O. Box 5100, Carlsbad, CA 92018-5100
(760) 431-7695 or (800) 654-5126
(760) 431-6948 (fax) or (800) 650-5115 (fax)
www.hayhouse.com® • www.hayfoundation.org

———

Published in Australia by: Hay House Australia Pty. Ltd.,
18/36 Ralph St., Alexandria NSW 2015
Phone: 612-9669-4299 • *Fax:* 612-9669-4144
www.hayhouse.com.au

Published in the United Kingdom by: Hay House UK, Ltd.,
The Sixth Floor, Watson House, 54 Baker Street, London W1U 7BU
Phone: +44 (0)20 3927 7290 • *Fax:* +44 (0)20 3927 7291
www.hayhouse.co.uk

Published in India by: Hay House Publishers India,
Muskaan Complex, Plot No. 3, B-2, Vasant Kunj, New Delhi 110 070
Phone: 91-11-4176-1620 • *Fax:* 91-11-4176-1630
www.hayhouse.co.in

———

Access New Knowledge.
Anytime. Anywhere.

Learn and evolve at your own pace
with the world's leading experts.

www.hayhouseU.com